Microprocessors Your Questions Answered

Alec Wood

Newnes Technical Books

Newnes Technical Books
is an imprint of the Butterworth Group
which has principal offices in
London, Sydney, Toronto, Wellington, Durban and Boston

First published 1982

© **Butterworths & Co. (Publishers) Ltd, 1982**
Borough Green, Sevenoaks, Kent TN15 8PH, England

British Library Cataloguing in Publication Data

Wood, Alec
    Microprocessors
    1. Microprocessors, microelectronics
    I. Title
    628.3819′58′35   TK7895.M5

    ISBN 0-408-00580-7

Photoset by Butterworths Litho Preparation Department
Printed in England by Billing & Son Ltd., Guildford

Preface

Ever since the BBC Horizon programme – Now the Chips are Down – 'microprocessor' has become a household word. However, entering the world of microcomputers is often a confusing experience due to the proliferation of 'new' ideas and jargon.

The aim of this short book is to answer as many as possible of the questions posed by the newcomer to microcomputing. I hope that both student and enthusiast will find this book useful before turning to more specialist hardware or software works, and that it will then also continue to be useful as a quick reference source.

The latest technology eight-bit microprocessors are covered but the general principles are equally applicable to microprocessors of any word length. No specific micro's instruction set is used as such. Instead I have attempted to show how you can refer to and use any real instruction set. I hope that even the dedicated high level language user will find it of interest to discover what goes on inside his micro.

A.W.

Contents

1
Silicon chips

What are microprocessors and why are they so important?

Microprocessors are the heart of a computer produced as a single electronic component. They have made it possible for microcomputers to go where no computer has gone before, out into the real world.

The microprocessor is a part of the environment it controls instead of being separate from it like the original mainframe, or later minicomputers. Already dedicated-task microprocessors (ones that can only perform the one job that the manufacturers programmed them to do) can be found in the home in TV games, toys, telephone charge calculators and other electrical goods. They will soon be found in most homes inside washing machines, television sets, stereo equipment, central heating and alarm systems; in fact in any suitable control situation where their inclusion will result in an optimising of performance or saving in the use of conventional components.

The latest television games can be 're-programmed' with different games' instructions contained in plug-in 'memory modules'. Some can even be programmed by the user.

Perhaps the most exciting present use of the user-programmable microprocessor is in the personal computer. It is now possible for the individual to own and use a computer which is compact and inexpensive. The microprocessor is the heart of the microcomputer, acting as its central processing unit (CPU). It is possible because recent advances in semiconductor technology have allowed the concentration of electronic circuits of enormous complexity into a very small space at very low cost and with the consumption of very little power.

Circuits of this type, known as semiconductor chips, first appeared in most homes inside pocket calculators, then in digital watches and now in microcomputers.

A microcomputer consists of the microprocessor chip and several other chips for such things as memory, and input and output control.

1

When semiconductors were first invented they were only pack-aged individually as discrete transistors, diodes, etc. In 1958, however, the integrated circuit (IC) was invented. This is a complete electronic circuit containing transistors and perhaps diodes, resistors, and capacitors produced entirely on a single chip of silicon, and is often less than a tenth of an inch square.

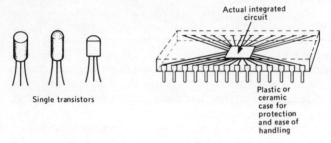

Fig. 1.1. Single transistors (left) and (right) a DIL (dual-in-line pack) in this case a 28 pin variety

The advantages of integrated circuits over discrete components lie in their small size, low cost and high reliability. Without such miniaturisation the personal computer would not have been possible for not only does it reduce the physical dimensions to manageable proportions and save money on cabinets, wire and space, but small circuits consume less power and speed up calculations as the electrical signals don't have so far to travel! This also simplifies the control of the various parts of the computer.

Why are microprocessors so inexpensive?

The cost savings resulting from integrated circuits are not only because of their smaller size. A large part of the saving is in the manufacture of the chips themselves. Once the circuit has been designed and the manufacturing equipment set up there is little difference in the production costs of a circuit containing ten active components and one containing 10 000 provided they are on the same size silicon chip. Roughly the same number of manufacturing steps are required in each case so the manufacturing costs are about the same. This means the heart of a computer, the microprocessor, can now be purchased for the same price as individual transistors first cost.

How many components can be placed on one chip?

At first it was only possible to manufacture a few active elements in one integrated circuit, perhaps a maximum of ten. This was known as small scale integration (SSI). Later, up to one hundred active elements on one chip were achieved and this was known as medium scale integration (MSI). Now we can manfuacture far more than this number in one integrated circuit and anything over one hundred is known as large scale integration (LSI).

Thirty-thousand active elements have been manufactured on a quarter-inch-square chip and it is expected to be able to achieve one million by 1985. The term Very Large Scale Integration (VLSI) is sometimes used for chips with thousands of active elements. You will be able to put this is in its true perspective if you realise that in the 1950s a typical electronic computer contained about 4000 valves and these had to be replaced at a rate of about forty a week. It used to be reckoned that the cost of a computer was proportional to the square of its power but with microcomputers this rule has been shattered. Personal computers today, costing less than one thousand pounds, are more powerful than computers costing many hundreds of thousands of pounds only a few years ago.

What exactly is a large scale integrated circuit?

A large scale integrated circuit is a complete electronic circuit manufactured in one package. There are two basic types of integrated circuits. Those which amplify and are used in audio equipment and other linear circuits and those which switch and are used in microprocessors and other digital circuits.

To understand microprocessors we need only concern ourselves with digital circuits. The components that are required in the integrated circuit are switches (transistors), perhaps a method of limiting the electric current that flows (resistors), something to store charge for future use (capacitors), and something to allow charge (current) to move in only one direction (diodes).

What are DTL, TTL, NMOS, PMOS and CMOS?

Some of the first digital integrated circuits used diodes and transistors as their main elements (gates) and this type of logic is known as diode transistor logic (DTL). Later devices used special transistors in place of the diodes and these circuits are known as transistor-transistor logic (TTL). Single chip microprocessors were made possible by the extra miniaturisation that came with the introduction of field effect transistors (FETs), of a special type known as Metal Oxide Semiconductor Transistors (MOSFETs). These do not work in the same way as conventional transistors used in transistor-transistor logic and are easier to understand than conventional bipolar transistors. MOSFETs can be used to amplify just like bipolar transistors can, but in microprocessors we are only interested in their switching properties.

There are two main ways of making MOSFETs. One way produces switches that are normally *on* and are turned *off* by the effect of an electric field produced by a voltage applied to one of their terminals (the gate). These are called depletion-type MOSFETs.

The other type are easier to manufacture using large scale integration techniques and are more common in microcomputers. They are called enhancement mode MOSFETs. They are normally *off* and turned *on* (enhanced) by a voltage applied to one of their terminals (the gate).

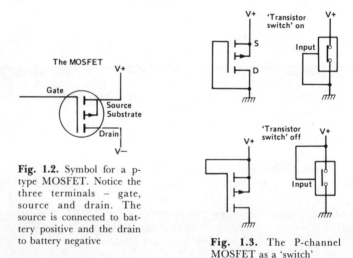

The MOSFET

Fig. 1.2. Symbol for a p-type MOSFET. Notice the three terminals – gate, source and drain. The source is connected to battery positive and the drain to battery negative

Fig. 1.3. The P-channel MOSFET as a 'switch'

There are also two subdivisions of the two types which are called P channel and N channel. Fig. 1.2 shows the circuit symbol for a P channel enhancement mode MOSFET.

Charges only flow through the P channel MOSFET if the gate is connected to a voltage that is negative compared to the substrate

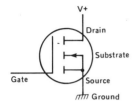

Fig. 1.4. An N-type MOSFET

(the silicon chip on which the transistor is built), which in a P channel MOSFET is connected to V+.

The P channel MOSFET therefore is switched ON if the gate is connected to ground (zero volts) and is OFF if the gate is connected to V+, or is unconnected.

P-channel enhancement mode
MOSFET

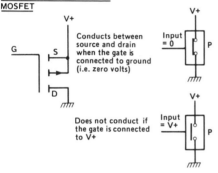

Conducts between source and drain when the gate is connected to ground (i.e. zero volts)

Does not conduct if the gate is connected to V+

N-channel enhancement mode
MOSFET

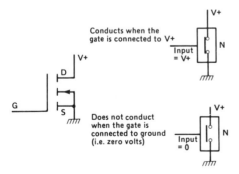

Conducts when the gate is connected to V+

Does not conduct when the gate is connected to ground (i.e. zero volts)

Fig. 1.5. Summary

Fig. 1.4 shows an N channel enhancement mode MOSFET. The N channel MOSFET is two N regions diffused into a P-type

5

substrate. Electrons are unable to conduct from the source to the drain unless the gate is this time made positive with repect to the substrate. If the gate is made negative with respect to the substrate the transistor is OFF.

Notice that in both types of MOSFET current does not flow continuously into or out of the gate. It is the voltage or field that turns the MOSFET on or off. Hence the name Field Effect Transistor. If you wish to find out more about integrated circuit techniques and the mechanisms of transistors these are covered in *Questions and Answers on Integrated Circuits* and *Questions and Answers on Transistors*, published by Newnes Technical Books.

Both types of MOSFETs can be used to make up logic circuits where they act as the switches. When they are ON their resistance is virtually zero and when they are OFF it is about a million-million ohms. However, they can also be used as resistors. If the channel is made longer and narrower than usual and the transistor gate connected so as to keep the MOSFET on, it will allow current to pass but will offer a resistance to it.

The MOSFET gate can also be used to store charge because no current flows from it into the channel due to the very good electrical insulating properties of the silicon oxide layer between them.

How are MOSFETs used in integrated circuits?

Integrated circuits are made by producing all the components and interconnecting links on the same substrate chip at the same time.

The chip may be no more than a quarter of an inch square and would be difficult to handle and easily damaged, so it is encased in plastic or ceramic and the connections are usually brought out to two rows of pins along the sides of the package. The pin arrangement is called Dual-In-Line (DIL) and the package is called a Dual-In-Line Package (DIP). Common chips have 8, 14, 16, 24, 28 or 40 pins in two rows each of 4, 7, 8, 12, 14 or 20. Most microprocessors are in 40-pin dual-in-line packages.

The circuits on some chips are made up of complementary pairs of P and N type MOSFETs. These are known as Complementary Metal Oxide Semiconductor chips (CMOS). You can also buy chips whose circuits use only P-type MOSFETs known as PMOS chips and others that use only N-type MOSFETs known as NMOS chips.

Common microprocessor chips are usually CMOS or NMOS. You will also find other smaller chips used alongside the microprocessor and some of these might well be transistor-transistor logic (TTL) chips. *Questions and Answers on Integrated Circuits* gives details of the different IC technologies and explains the diffusion techniques by which they are manufactured.

Why have MOSFETs allowed greater miniaturisation than TTL?

The MOSFET takes up less room on a chip than a bipolar transistor, since only one diffusion is required to place the drain and

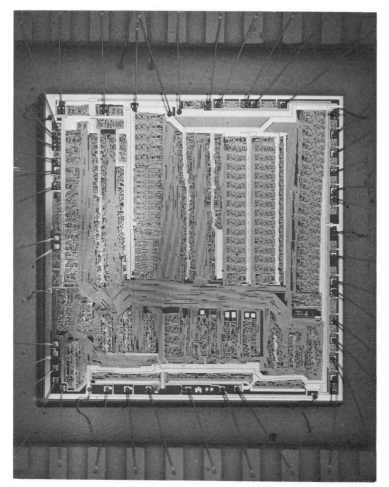

Fig. 1.6. The lid off a microprocessor

source of a MOSFET on the chip. A bipolar transistor requires three and takes up more room because each diffusion has to be inside the last.

Greater miniaturisation is also achieved because MOSFET circuits are much simpler than TTL circuits and use fewer components than the equivalent bipolar circuits (TTL).

Resistors are easy to achieve with MOSFETs, as already described. They take up very little extra space but diffused resistors used in bipolar chips take up far more room.

Integrated circuit manufacturing techniques lend themselves to producing the same basic unit over and over again and this is how manufacturers like to make up their circuits. If you examine a silicon chip through a microscope you will see regular repeating patterns of the same basic units (see Fig. 1.6).

How is switching achieved?

CMOS circuits are the easiest for the newcomer to electronics to understand and these will be used to describe how the various parts of a microcomputer function. The basic CMOS unit is the inverter switch and by combining these together in different ways we will see how any part of a microcomputer can be made.

Before we examine the circuit diagram of a CMOS inverter, let's look at a simplified switch circuit of what an inverter does. An inverter can be thought of as a ganged switch in a box connected between the output and *EITHER* V+ *OR* ground. (Ganged means both parts move together as if connected by some sort of lever.)

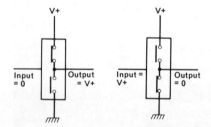

Fig. 1.7. The inverter as a switch

If the input is connected to ground (zero) the switch connects the output to V+. If the input is connected to V+ the output is connected to ground (zero). Fig. 1.7 shows this.

If this was a mechanical switch you could think of it as being operated by electromagnets and returned by some form of spring. You can see that the output is always the opposite of the input. That is, it is inverted.

8

However, microcomputers do not use electromagnetic or mechanical switches, they use transistors to switch. The basic CMOS inverter is shown in Fig. 1.8 next to our mechanical switch inverter.

You should be able to identify the P and N-type transistors that act as the switches. The gates are connected together, therefore when one transistor is on the other must be off. This is because when the input is V+ both gates are at V+ so this turns the N channel FET ON and the P channel FET OFF, and the output is connected to ground (zero) via the N channel FET.

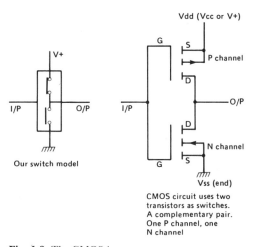

CMOS circuit uses two transistors as switches. A complementary pair. One P channel, one N channel

Fig. 1.8. The CMOS inverter

When the gates are connected to ground (zero) the N channel FET is OFF and the P channel FET is ON, so the output is connected to V+ via the P channel FET.

Fig. 1.9 shows TTL, PMOS and NMOS inverter circuits. You will come across NMOS and perhaps PMOS circuits so, remembering how the CMOS circuit worked, let's simplify the NMOS and PMOS inverters to 'switch circuits' and see how they operate.

The PMOS inverter can be considered as a switch between V+ and the output, and a resistor between the output and ground. When the input is zero the switch is closed and the output is at V+. When the input is connected to V+ the switch opens and the output is connected to ground by the resistor. If very little, or no, current flows, for instance if the output is connected to the gate of another MOSFET, the output is at zero volts.

9

Now look at Fig. 1.10 and see if you can visualise the transistor switching the output as the input changes.

Now consider the NMOS inverter shown in Fig. 1.11. This can be considered as a resistor between V+ and the output and a switch between the output and ground. When the input is zero the switch is open and the output is connected to V+ via the resistor. If the current is small, or no current flows, as when the output is connected to the gate of another MOSFET, then the voltage at the output will be V+. When the input is connected to V+ the switch closes and the output is connected to ground.

Look at Fig. 1.11 and see if you can visualise the transistor switching the output as the input changes.

The reason that you will come across CMOS, PMOS and NMOS circuits in microcomputers is that there are advantages and dis-

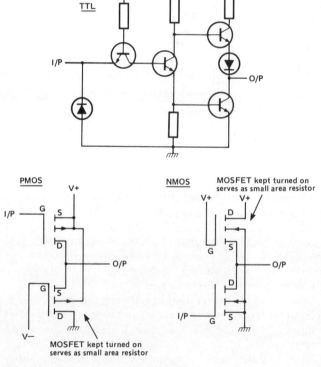

Fig. 1.9. TTL, PMOS and NMOS inverters

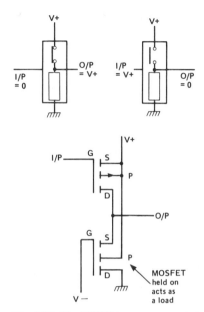

Fig. 1.10. The PMOS inverter as a switch

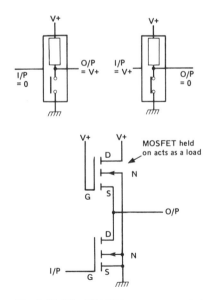

Fig. 1.11. The NMOS inverter as a switch

11

advantages peculiar to each. At the moment the most common are NMOS and CMOS. NMOS circuits consume more power than CMOS due to the 'resistors' taking power even when the output is zero. CMOS power requirements, on the other hand, are less stringent as no power is consumed by the switches themselves. PMOS switches are the slowest and are being used less frequently.

When the various parts of a microcomputer are introduced, we will discuss them in terms of the CMOS inverter so that newcomers to electronics will not have to worry about any components other than switches. You should find it easy to visualise the equivalent NMOS or PMOS circuit yourself if you wish.

2
Hardware and its terminology

What microprocessors am I likely to come across?

There are many different microprocessors available from several manufacturers but you will probably come across the 6502, the 6800, the Z80, and the 8080 as these are the most common microprocessors in personal computers.

The 6502 is a 40-pin dual-in-line package N-type metal oxide semiconductor (NMOS) chip, and is used in such microcomputers as KIM, Superboard, Challenger, Pet, Acorn and Apple II.

The 6800 is a 40-pin DIP NMOS chip and is used in such microcomputers as the 77-68 and the Southwest Technical Products 6800 Computer System.

The Z80 is also a 40-pin DIP NMOS chip and is used in such microcomputers as the Tandy TRS 80, the Exidy Sorcerer, Research Machine's 380Z, Tuscan and the Nascom microcomputers.

The 8080 is a forerunner of the Z80 and is used in the ABC 80, Triton and many other microcomputers.

The Z80 and 6502 are sometimes referred to as third generation microprocessors. This is because they belong to a family of microprocessors, each later member of the family being a development of those that went before.

An ideal situation would be to have one single microprocessor for all types of applications but as development is still taking place we are still a long way from this.

A common abbreviation for microprocessor unit is MPU, which means the microprocessor itself. A microcomputer uses an MPU as its central processing unit (CPU). The CPU controls and co-ordinates the activities of the rest of the microcomputer as well as performing all the arithmetic and logic processes, and routeing information from one unit to another.

There are two main 'family trees'.

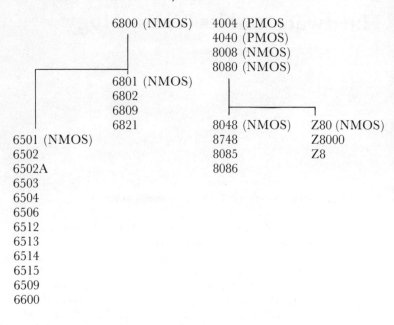

6800 (NMOS)

6801 (NMOS)
6802
6809
6821

6501 (NMOS)
6502
6502A
6503
6504
6506
6512
6513
6514
6515
6509
6600

4004 (PMOS
4040 (PMOS)
8008 (NMOS)
8080 (NMOS)

8048 (NMOS)   Z80 (NMOS)
8748   Z8000
8085   Z8
8086

What else is required to make a microcomputer apart from the microprocessor unit itself?

As well as the MPU a microcomputer also requires a memory in which to store information on how to control the user's program instructions. This type of memory is known as read only memory (ROM). The manufacturer programs it when he makes it and it can not then be altered by the user.

As well as ROM a microcomputer requires memory in which the user can store his own program instructions and data and from which the computer can then read under the control of the instructions in the ROM. This type of read/write memory is known as RAM. This originally stood for random access memory but read only memory is also random access; that is, it does not have to be read in serial form like a tape cassette. We can go to any part of it in any order like turning to a page in a reference book.

Think of ROM as read only memory and RAM as read and write memory.

What are microcomputer peripherals and ports?

A microcomputer also requires input and output ports to connect up to external devices called peripherals, such as a keyboard, a TV monitor, or a printer which prints your output on paper (hard copy). These ports are also referred to as interfaces and you will probably come across most of the following: ACIA, UART, RS232 interface, Kansas City cassette interface, and IEEE-488 instrument interface.

What is a bus?

The lines that carry data between the different parts of the microcomputer are called data lines. The complex of data lines is called a data bus. Microcomputers commonly have eight data lines in parallel connecting various parts so the data bus is said to be an eight-bit data bus. This is because each data line can carry one binary digit (bit) of information.

What does the clock do?

The microcomputer requires a clock generator to provide system timing to ensure that all the parts work in the correct sequence. Sometimes the clock circuit is on the MPU chip and only requires a few external components but some microprocessors require a complete external clock circuit.

How are signals sent to different parts of the computer?

The microcomputer also requires control and address lines so that instructions can be sent to the various parts of the microcomputer. These lines are usually separate from the data lines. There are normally 16 address lines which allow you to select any part of the memory, i.e. address it. The system of address lines is called the address bus.

The complete system of data, address, control and power lines is called the bus structure. There have been two main attempts to produce a standard layout of these lines so as to make it easier to connect together equipment from different manufacturers more easily. These are the S100 bus system and the E78 or europa bus system.

What is meant by hardware and software?

Hardware is the name given to the mechanical and electronic parts of the microcomputer. The microprocessor unit, the memory, the keyboard, the visual display unit (TV screen) are all hardware.

Software is the name given to the programs themselves. By changing the program in the microcomputer you can make the hardware behave in different ways. For instance, one program might turn your microcomputer into a television game, another a calculator, another a stock record or invoicing system, another a burglar alarm controller, and so on.

What are the different types of storage used in microcomputers?

The software usually has to be stored in a backing store, such as a tape recorder, and then fed into the microcomputer as required, because, except in certain dedicated control situations, you will be unlikely to have sufficient memory in your microcomputer to store and run all the programs you want to use. Even if you did, your computer would have to be switched on all the time because RAM loses its information when switched off and has to be programmed again (so it is said to be volatile).

ROM does not lose its information but you would not want to have all your programs in ROM because you would then be dependent on the manufacturer to make them for you. An alternative for programs you use frequently, perhaps to help you run or edit other programs, is a user-programmable read only memory called PROM. You program this once to your own specification and it is then just like read only memory. It is still rather expensive. It is also sometimes called electrically-programmable read only memory but *do not confuse this with EPROM*, which stands for erasable-programmable read only memory. This you can program in much the same way as programmable read only memory and then use as read only memory. If in the future you wish to change the contents of this type of memory there is a window in the top of it and, if it is exposed to ultraviolet light of the correct intensity and wavelength, the contents of the memory are erased and it can be programmed again. Sometimes this is also called UVEPROM.

So to sum up, software that you use with every program, such as the monitor program, is best stored in read only memory of one type or another. It is then sometimes called firmware (i.e. software firmly fixed in hardware).

Actual program software then has to be fed into the random access memory each time it is wanted. This software can be stored ready for use in several ways. It can be written down on paper and fed into the microcomputer via switches in a simple system, or some sort of keyboard in a more complex system. It can also be stored on magnetic tape (a backing store) and fed into the microcomputer via a special serial input port called an asynchronous communication interface adapter (ACIA) or sometimes a universal asynchronous receiver transmitter (UART) is used.

Tape interfaces are sometimes described as being to the CUTS or Kansas City standard. Kansas City refers to a particular method for storing data on tape based on the computer users' tape system (CUTS) which defines a series of tones to represent data in binary form as a series of 1s and 0s.

Special ports are required to enable the microcomputer to handle the data from a tape because although the microcomputer handles data in parallel form along each of its eight data lines at once, information can only come from the tape one bit at a time in serial form as it passes the tape head. Although transfer rates of 300 bits per second (300 baud) can be achieved with normal tape recorders and up to 1200 baud with a good recorder it can still take quite some time to load a program from a cassette, particularly if you have to scan through the whole cassette. (Note: 1 baud = 1 bit per second. You do not count any control signals sent as well, only the actual data for processing, addresses in memory, and instructions.)

A quicker but more expensive method is to store the information on a floppy disk or mini floppy. This is a sort of magnetic record which needs a lot of memory and other circuits to control it and a serial input/output port. Although information is still stored and read in serial form the disk has direct access almost immediately to any part and is much quicker than tape.

What other hardware am I likely to come across?

On the input side you will either have a bank of switches if the system is very simple or else some sort of keyboard. The simplest is called is a kexadecimal keyboard.

There are 16 keys for putting in program instructions, data for processing, and addresses. There will also be some control switches or keys to enable you to run the program.

A more complex keyboard is the full typewriter or QWERTY (the first six letters of the top row) keyboard.

When you press one of these keys the signal has to be converted into a code suitable for passing along the data bus. The code used is the American Standard Code for Information Interchange (ASCII).

Either type of keyboard is interfaced (connected) to the bus via an input port that handles data in parallel form. These interfaces are known as Peripheral Interface Adapters (PIA) or Parallel Input/Output (PIO) ports.

C	D	E	F
8	9	A	B
4	5	6	7
0	1	2	3

Fig. 2.1. A typical hexadecimal keyboard

These perform a similar function to the serial ports already mentioned but information is handled in parallel form (i.e. more than one bit at a time), whereas tape, teletype, and visual display unit (VDU) outputs, ACIAs and UARTs, convert the information to a serial form. You may think that you are seeing information on a TV screen all at once but this is an illusion. The picture is built up by a spot moving from one position to the next along each line of the picture in turn, so the displayed information is built up in serial form.

The data lines are usually buffered before they enter these ports. A buffer is a circuit that provides electrical isolation between one part of the system and another but at the same time passes on the data.

The simplest microcomputers of all do not require an output port and the data lines are just connected to light-emitting diodes (LEDs) via suitable buffers.

Some input and output devices have what is known as handshake facilities. This simply means that the peripheral and microprocessor unit are able to 'ask' each other if they are ready for data exchange and data is only transferred if the answer is 'yes'.

If you want your microcomputer to be able to exchange information with another computer some way away then you can do this via a telephone provided you have a modulator/demodulator called a MODEM which converts information from your peripheral interface adaptor into sound signals to send along the telephone lines via an acoustic coupler.

What would be a typical arrangement of hardware in a microcomputer?

The amount of hardware depends on how simple or complex a system is. One of the simplest systems is shown in Fig. 2.2.

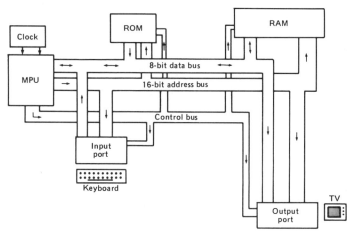

Fig. 2.2. A simple microcomputer system

3
Software and its terminology

What does software look like?

If written down or displayed on a visual display unit it is addresses (or line numbers), instructions and data in the form of words, codes, or numbers, depending on the programming language used.

For instance, many microcomputers can be programmed in a language called BASIC. This is known as a high level language. A program in BASIC to add two numbers together might look something like:

Line number	Instructions and data
01	LET A = 7
02	LET B = 11
03	LET C = A + B
04	PRINT C
05	END

The information cannot be understood by the microprocessor in this form so a special program, either an interpreter or a compiler, in the read only memory converts this into machine language to enable the program to be run.

The next step down from a high level language is assembly language and this can be used on a microcomputer with less memory because you are doing some of the work for it. A similar program to add two numbers in assembly language might look something like:

Mnemonic	Symbolic address in memory
LDA	compartment 102
ADC	compartment 203
STA	compartment 101
BRK	—

where LDA means load, ADC means add, STA means store and BRK means stop.

Although not shown here, the two numbers to be added have also to be entered into the memory at addresses compartment 102 and compartment 203.

A special program called an assembler program converts this into machine language to enable the program to be run.

The next step down is to program in hexadecimal code and this *has* to be done on less expensive microcomputers. You are doing even more work for the computer. A similar program to add two numbers might look like this in hexadecimal code:

Hex code for the operation	Address in memory referred to by the instruction
AD	11 00) again the actual
6D	CB 00) numbers have also
8D	65 00) to be entered into
00	– –) the memory.

A special program called a monitor program in the read only memory converts this into machine language when the program is entered.

If you have only the simplest of microcomputers with switches as inputs then you will probably have to enter your programs directly in machine language by means of the switches. A similar program to add two numbers might look like this in machine code (language):

Binary operation code	Address in memory referred to by instruction			
1010 1101	0110	0110	0000	0000
0011 1100	1100	1011	0000	0000
1000 1101	0110	0101	0000	0000
0000 0000	—	—	—	–

Each line, i.e. the op-code and the address referred to, if any, is called an instruction.

The op-codes used in this last example are those for the 6502 microprocessor. Its add instruction is an 'add with carry' which requires carries from previous calculations (the carry flag is explained later) to be cleared, if not required, before the add instruction is used. For simplicity, that instruction was omitted above but will be shown in future. Some microprocessors also have a separate 'add without carry' instruction and the carry flag does not have to be cleared before this instruction is used. We will use 'add with carry' instructions in the examples in this chapter and in a later chapter we will show how both types of instruction can be used if they are available on your microprocessor.

Unfortunately the operation codes for different microprocessors are different and if you are programming in the low level languages – hexadecimal or machine code – you must know the instruction set operation codes for the particular microprocessor that you are using.

Summary

High level language $(C = A + B)$ → compiler → machine language → microprocessor, is 5 times faster than:
Assembly language (mnemonic) → assembler → machine language → microprocessor, is 10 times faster than:
Hexadecimal programming (FF etc) → monitor → machine language → microprocessor, is 4 times faster than:
Binary machine language (0010 etc) → loader → microprocessor

It can be seen that programming in a high level language is about five times faster than in assembly language, or (5×10) fifty times faster than programming in hexadecimal, or $(5 \times 10 \times 4)$ 200 times faster than programming in machine language.

Why does the hardware need its instructions in machine code?

As we have already seen the hardware is really very simple since it is just made up of lots of switches and these can only handle the two electrical states ON and OFF. It would be very difficult to design a reliable electrical system that would detect ten voltage levels used to represent the numbers 0 to 9 in normal decimal counting. The software, therefore, has to reduce every problem to a series of ONs and OFFs and therefore has to use only two digits (usually 0 for OFF and 1 for ON).

The microprocessor counts in what would to a human be a very clumsy way – the binary system. This uses the base 2 instead of base 10 which means we carry to the next column whenever the column total reaches 2 just as in decimal we carry to the next column every time the column total reaches 10.

So starting at zero and counting up one number at a time in binary gives:

Start	0000
add one, gives	0001

This time when we add one we have to carry

  this gives   0010

  add one, gives   0011

This time when we add one we have to carry again, and again in the second column:

                      0100

and so on. Decimal numbers 0 to 15 are shown here with the equivalent binary numbers:

Decimal	Binary
0	0000
1	0001
2	0010
3	0011
4	0100
5	0101
6	0110
7	0111
8	1000
9	1001
10	1010
11	1011
12	1100
13	1101
14	1110
15	1111

Notice that each binary digit (bit) stands for a power of 2. The right-most digit, the least significant, stands for $2^0 = 1$, the next $2^1 = 2$, the next $2^2 = 4$, the next $2^3 = 8$, the next $2^4 = 16$, then $2^5 = 32$, then $2^6 = 64$, then $2^7 = 128$ and so on.

Thus 1101 is the binary for 13 because

$$\frac{8\,4\,2\,1}{1\,1\,0\,1}$$

binary

We have:

one 8 = 8

one 4 = 4

no 2 = 0

one 1 = 1

which is 13 in decimal

and   01100010 stands for

128	64	32	16	8	4	2	1

binary   0   1   1   0   0   0   1   0

one 64 = 64
one 32 = 32
one 2 = 2

which is   98 in decimal.

Each binary digit, 0 or 1, is called a bit. The hardware treats a voltage of V+ as a 1 and zero voltage as a 0. This is known as positive logic. As we have already seen, the hardware handles multiples of eight bits at a time along its buses, eight bits along the data bus and 16 bits along the address bus. Multiples of eight bits are referred to as words. An eight-bit word is called a byte and 2^{10} bytes (1024) is often referred to as a kilobyte.

Some earlier first-generation microprocessors such as the 4004 and 4040 only had four-bit data buses. A four-bit word is called a nibble.

You should now be able to see why a microprocessor with a 16-bit address bus can address anything up to 64 K of memory. The 16 address lines allow any address from 0000 0000 0000 0000 up to 1111 1111 1111 1111. In decimal this is from 0 to 65 535. In other words, with a 16-bit address bus if you include the address 0 there are 65 536 different addresses, or places in memory, possible. This is 64×1024 or 64 K. Notice that 65 536 is 2^{16}. In general n address lines can address 2^n locations.

Of course not all microcomputers have sufficient memory to utilise all these 65 536 possible addresses.

Why don't we program in binary all the time?

The microprocessor can only sense two voltage levels, V+ and zero, so it must have all its instructions and data presented to it in this way, i.e. in binary form (machine language).

We find it clumsy to write in binary form and so we like to write programs in various other codes and we use a program in the read only memory to convert these codes into binary form for us.

Why do we use hexadecimal?

In some ways, if you really want to know what is going on inside your microcomputer, hexadecimal is a good code to use because it allows you to keep track of the 1s and the 0s without the bother of writing them out all the time.

Hexadecimal code uses the base 16 and the letters A, B, C, D, E, F, to represent 10, 11, 12, 13, 14 and 15 respectively.

Compare decimal 0 to 15 with binary and hexadecimal:

Decimal	Binary	Hex
0	0000	0
1	0001	1
2	0010	2
3	0011	3
4	0100	4
5	0101	5
6	0110	6
7	0111	7
8	1000	8
9	1001	9
10	1010	A
11	1011	B
12	1100	C
13	1101	D
14	1110	E
15	1111	F

Therefore decimal 11 is written as 1011 in binary and as B in hex.

How does this help? It just appears more complicated to me!

If you had to copy out the 16 bit binary number 1101001010111110 (try it on a scrap of paper) as part of a program you would find it much easier to break it down into four-bit nibbles:

1101   0010   1011   1110

Then, instead, write the hex code for each section:

1101   0010   1011   1110
D   2   B   E
= D2BE

This is much easier to copy down accurately, and in the case of codes that represent operations, hex is easier to remember than strings of 0s and 1s.

If you want to write a program then you can now do it in hexadecimal with comparative ease.

How do I write a program in hexadecimal?

The first thing to do is to get hold of a copy of the repertoire of the things the microprocessor can do along with the operation codes that cause it to do them. This is called the instruction set for the microprocessor and should be supplied with it when you buy it.

Here are some instructions for a 'typical microprocessor' along with the hexadecimal op-codes representing the binary codes that cause the microprocessor to execute the instructions, i.e. set the right sequence of 'switches' to channel the information to the correct places and process it:

Instruction meaning	Hex code
LOAD the contents of the memory address I specify directly after this op-code into a space (a register) in the MPU called the accumulator.	AD
ADD (with carry) the contents of the memory address I specify directly after this op-code to the contents of the accumulator and then put the answer in the accumulator instead of the number that is already there.	6D
STORE the contents of the accumulator at the address in memory I specify directly after this op-code.	8D
STOP.	00
CLEAR the part of the MPU that stores the carries of any carry-overs from previous calculations. (Carry flag.)	18

So let's see if we can write a real program to add two numbers together. Before we write it in hex let's see if we can imagine in our minds what is going to take place inside the microcomputer. Think of the microcomputer as four main units, INPUT, OUTPUT, MICROPROCESSOR UNIT and MEMORY.

Think of the microprocessor unit as having three sections:

1. temporary stores called registers
2. the arithmetic and logic unit (ALU) that performs the arithmetic and logic, rather like a calculator
3. the control unit.

Think of the memory as a rack or silo consisting of numbered compartments. The numbers represent the address of the memory

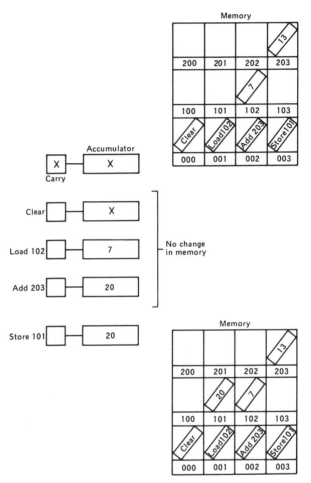

Fig. 3.1. The 'rack' model showing the program instructions in compartments 0 to 3 and the numbers to be added in compartments 102 and 103. After the program has been run the answer is in compartment 101

location represented by the compartment. The memory is used to store both the program data and the instructions.

The control unit, as its name suggests, controls all the other units and ensures that the program instructions are executed one at a time.

What must our program do? First assume that we have already put the two numbers to be added in the memory in compartments 102 and 203.

27

Now we must clear any carry-overs from previous calculations. Then we must copy the data in compartment 102 into the accumulator in the ALU. Next we must copy the data in compartment 203 into the ALU and add it to the data already there. Finally we must copy the answer back into the memory store; say into compartment 101.

Data in memory is not destroyed when it is read. It is simply copied. Data will remain in memory until another number is read in its place or the power is turned off.

Our instructions are: CLEAR – the carry flag
LOAD (the data in compartment) 102
ADD (the data in compartment) 203
STORE (the answer in compartment) 101.

Written in hexadecimal to run on our 'typical microcomputer' with a hex keyboard, these instructions would be built up as follows:

Get rid of any carry-overs from previous calculations which will be:

18 in hex

The next thing we must do is copy or fetch the first number from the memory and place it in a temporary store (the accumulator) inside the microprocessor unit itself. So the next instruction in hex is AD:

18
AD

But that instruction says that we will specify the memory location in which the data we want is stored. Let that be address 0066 in hex (decimal 102). So this address has to be written after the op-code with the least significant digits first, i.e. as 66 00. (Don't worry about it being back to front, i.e. low byte first. By always putting the low byte first, instructions that don't require the high order byte execute faster.):

18
AD 66 00

Next we must add to this number a number that is contained in another memory location (say 00 CB hex which is decimal 203). So the next instruction is 6D followed by the memory location with the least significant digits first (CB 00):

18
AD 66 00
6D CB 00

Next we wish to put the answer which is now in the accumulator back into a place in memory (say 0065 hex which is decimal 101), so the next instruction is 8D followed by 65 00:

18
AD 66 00
6D CB 00
8D 65 00

So we now have the program on paper and it has to be entered into the computer. We do this by entering instructions into consecutive addresses in the memory so that when the MPU's control circuit takes over control, it can count through the program step by step.

So, returning to our model, we would put the instruction CLEAR in compartment 000, LOAD 102 in compartment 001, ADD 203 in compartment 002, and STORE 101 in compartment 003.

Of course you must also enter the data (the numbers to be added) in the locations specified in the program instructions, i.e. compartments 102 and 203 (see Fig. 3.1).

It is almost as easy in hex. The program was:

18
AD 66 00
6D CB 00
8D 65 00

You will see later that each memory location in the microcomputer can store only eight binary digits, but, as we saw before, each pair of hex digits above represents eight binary digits. For instance, 18 represents:

1	8
0001	1000

or the eight-bit binary word 00011000. So we can store the first instruction in one memory location, say compartment 000 decimal, which is also 0000 in hex. However, the next instruction in hex, the op-code AD, and the address in hex 66 00, require three locations in memory; 0001, 0002 and 0003. The next instruction 6D CB 00 requires the next three memory locations 0004, 0005 and 0006 and the next instruction 8D 65 00 requires the next three memory locations 0007, 0008 and 0009 (in hex).

We should also then add a stop instruction, which from the instruction set table is found to be 00. This should be placed in the next memory location 000A.

The two numbers to be added, say decimal 7 (07 hex) and decimal 13 (0D hex), have also to be entered in the memory locations specified in the program which were 0066 hex and 00CB hex. We can now hand control over to the microcomputer monitor program by pressing the RUN or GO switch after carrying out any other control steps required by the particular microcomputer, for instance telling it where to find the start of our program. To see what happens think of the model again

The control circuitry includes a program counter and this is used to enable the control unit to fetch the first instruction from the first memory location, execute it, and then fetch the second instruction, execute that, and so on until it reaches the end of the program when it stops.

If we now read the contents of compartment 101 we find the answer there.

We could now change the data at 102 and 203 and run the program again to perform the addition of two different numbers.

Written down, the memory addresses where the instructions are stored and the actual operation codes and addresses referred to by them, would look like this in our model:

Memory address where instruction stored	Operation 'code'	Address referred to in instruction
000	CLEAR	—
001	LOAD	compartment 102
002	ADD	compartment 203
003	STORE	compartment 101
004	STOP	—

Applying the same idea to our hex program we get:

Memory address where op-code is stored	Op codes (operand)	Address referred to in instructions (arguments)	
0000	18	—	—
0001	AD	66	00
0004	6D	CB	00
0007	8D	65	00
000A	00	—	—

The two numbers we wish to add, 07 hex and
0D hex must be placed in memory locations
0066 and 00CB. The answer is read from 0065

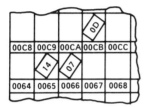

Note. Decimal 20 = hex 14

Fig. 3.2. The 'rack' model with hex codes

You should be able to follow this reasonably well. If you are
uncertain about any of it then read this section again. In a later
chapter we will explain how a program like this is fetched from
memory and used to control the various parts of the microcomputer.
Many people have to write their programs in this way because their
microcomputer has only a hexadecimal keyboard.

Why are assemblers used?

As your programs become longer it becomes more and more difficult
to remember the codes for the different operations and more and
more tedious keeping lists of addresses of the stored or computed
data. If when it is written you find you have to change or edit the
program it can be a real headache sorting all the addresses out
again.

It is therefore much easier to write your programs in mnemonic
assembly language. You then feed it in in that form and an
assembler program converts all your mnemonics and addresses into
machine language, places the resulting machine language program
in the correct order in the memory and also takes care of all the
addresses used by the program.

Assembler programs can be obtained resident in read only
memory or on tape for reading into your microcomputer's random

access memory each time you want to use it. You can also write your own assembler program of course!

Why are high level languages used?

With a high level language such as BASIC then you have even fewer problems because memory locations don't worry you at all. The compiler or interpreter program takes care of these and also allows you to use a code for your instructions that looks almost like English. Several instructions can also be grouped together as statements on one line.

In BASIC adding two numbers becomes one simple statement:

LET C = A + B

You can even get the answer displayed, without knowing where in the memory it is stored, by using the instruction:

PRINT C

A complete program, including the input of data and printing the answer, would be:

10 LET	A = 7	Note: it is convention
20 LET	B = 13	to number lines in tens
30 LET	C = A + B	so that it is easy to go
40 PRINT	C	back and insert lines if
50 END		you make a mistake.

This is entered at the keyboard and is usually executed by typing the command RUN.

Almost at once 20 – the value of C – is printed on the next line.

So what? I could have added 7 to 13 faster in my head

Yes, but the simple programs used so far have only been intended to illustrate how data can be placed in the memory and then moved around and processed as required. Even a simple calculator can do that! What makes the microcomputer so much more powerful is its ability to follow not only a set pattern of arithmetic instructions but also logic, comparison and conditional or decision-making instructions that enable different paths to be taken through the program.

4
Logic

If a microcomputer is only a lot of simple switches then how can it perform arithmetic, logic, comparison, and decision-making operations?

Believe it or not, the logic and decision-making operations are the easiest to understand. Logical relationships are expressed in Boolean algebra, invented in 1854 by G. Boole, for studying human reasoning processes. It was later adapted to analyse electrical switching circuits. There are five basic operations: NOT, AND, OR, NAND, and NOR. Each can be implemented electronically with logic gates. The different logic gates can be interconnected in different ways to provide complex functions for adding, subtracting, comparing etc.

Let's examine the five basic logic operations one at a time and see how they can be implemented with simple switches. Don't try to convert these into transistor circuits yet because once you understand the logic operations there are a few tricks that will enable you to build any of them up from just one basic CMOS circuit.

What is a NOT gate?

Complementation or inversion (NOT) is denoted by a bar above the quantity to be inverted. So 'NOT A' is written as $\bar{A}$.

Our hardware can only handle two logic states, $V+$ which represents a 1, and zero volts which represents a 0 in positive logic. Therefore if A is 0, NOT A must be 1 and vice versa. The logic symbol for a NOT gate (or inverter) is shown in Fig. 4.1.

The NOT operation can be thought of as a ganged switch in a box between the output and either $V+$ or ground. If the input is zero the switch connects the output to $V+$ (logic 1). If the input is $V+$ the output will be zero.

As with all the logic in this chapter the output depends only on the present input and it changes as the input changes. This is known as combinational logic.

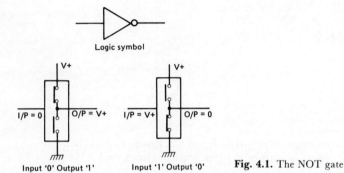

Logic symbol

Input '0' Output '1'   Input '1' Output '0'   **Fig. 4.1.** The NOT gate

We can plot an input-output table called a truth table for gates to help us understand the logic operations that can be carried out with them. The table for a NOT operation is:

input-output table

input	output
0	V+
V+	0

logic truth table

A	Ā
0	1
1	0

We get the input-output table by simply listing all possible inputs and then writing the corresponding outputs next to them.

Not strictly a logic operation but something you will come across a lot is the BUFFER. Its symbol is shown in Fig. 4.2. This is the opposite of a NOT operation and simply provides electrical isolation between input and output.

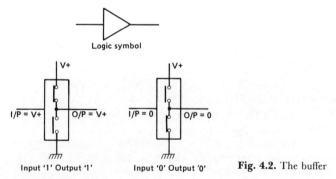

Logic symbol

Input '1' Output '1'   Input '0' Output '0'   **Fig. 4.2.** The buffer

Think of a buffer as a switch in a box like the inverter but this time when the input is V+ the output is also V+. When the input is zero the output is switched to zero. The truth table for a buffer is:

34

input	output
0	0
1	1

What is an AND gate?

The AND operation is denoted by a dot · which is read as AND. A·B means A and B.

The AND gate only gives an output if the inputs are A and B together. The logic symbol for an AND gate is shown in Fig. 4.3.

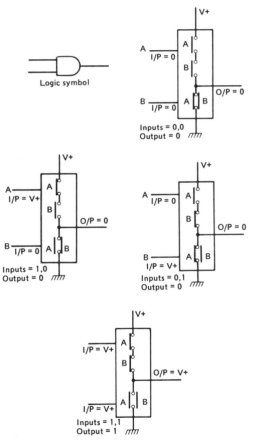

Fig. 4.3. The AND gate

The AND operation can be thought of as two buffers in the same box with their switches between V+ and the output connected one after the other in series, and their switches between ground and the output side by side in parallel. Notice that as the switches are buffers an input of zero closes the appropriate switch to ground to give a zero output.

If input A is V+ the output still remains at zero even though the top switch closes and one of the bottom switches opens. Similarly if B is V+ and A is zero. But if A AND B are both V+ at the same time the output is connected to V+ too.

Hence the name an AND operation. The truth table for an AND operation is:

A	B	A AND B
0	0	0
0	1	0
1	0	0
1	1	1

What is an OR gate?

The OR operation is denoted by a + which is read as OR. In Boolean algebra A + B means A OR B. An OR gate gives an output if either A OR B are present at the inputs.

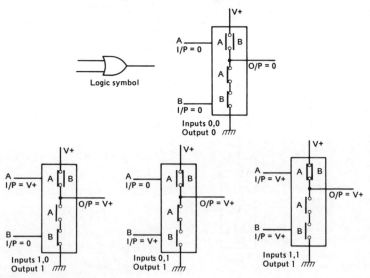

Fig. 4.4. The OR gate

36

The logic symbol for an OR gate is shown in Fig. 4.4.

The OR operation can be thought of as two buffers in the same box but this time with their switches between V+ and the output in parallel, and their switches between ground and the output in series.

If either A OR B is now V+ the output is connected to V+. Notice that the condition when *both* A and B are V+ is not excluded and the output is still V+.

Hence the name OR operation because the output is V+ if either A OR B separately or together is V+. The truth table for the OR operation is:

A	B	A OR B
0	0	0
0	1	1
1	0	1
1	1	1

What is a NAND gate?

The NAND operation stands for NOT AND and is denoted by $\overline{A.B}$. A NAND gate does not give an output when the input is A and B together. The symbol for a NAND gate is shown in Fig. 4.5.

The NAND operation can be thought of as two inverters in the same box with their switches between V+ and the output in parallel, and with their switches between ground and the ouput in series. Notice that as the switches are inverters a zero input closes the appropriate switch to V+ and gives an output of V+. The OR operation was similar but used buffers.

If either A or B is now set individually to V+ the output remains as it is, at V+. But if A and B are set to V+ at the same time the output becomes connected to ground. Hence the name NOT A AND B, or NAND.

The truth table for the NAND operation is:

A	B	A NAND B
0	0	1
0	1	1
1	0	1
1	1	0

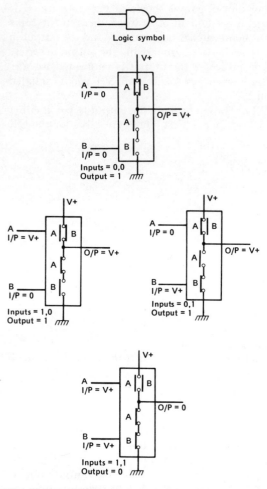

Fig. 4.5. The NAND gate

What is a NOR gate?

The NOR operation stands for NOT OR and is written $\overline{A+B}$ meaning NOT A OR B. In other words it does not give an output when the input is either A or B. The symbol for a NOR gate is shown in Fig. 4.6.

The NOR operation can be thought of as two inverters in the same box but this time with their switches between V+ and the

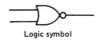

Logic symbol

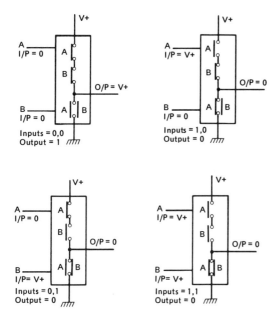

Fig. 4.6. The NOR gate

output in series, and their switches between ground and the output in parallel. Notice that as the switches are inverters a zero input closes the appropriate switch to V+. This is different from the model of an AND operation which looks similar but uses buffers.

If either A or B are now connected, individually or together, to V+ the output becomes connected to ground. Hence the name NOT A OR B or NOR.

The truth table for the NOR operation is:

A	B	A NOR B
0	0	1
0	1	0
1	0	0
1	1	0

There are so many operations I am getting confused. Can't we simplify things a bit?

Yes, provided you understand the logic operations so far. In reality, we don't need to make a separate electronic gate to perform each separate logic operation.

Large scale integration lends itself to producing large numbers of *the same* basic unit over and over again on one chip. One simplification is to use the inverter as a basic building block. Both the NAND and NOR gates can be made up from 'two inverters' as we have already seen. By combining NAND and NOR gates and more inverters, any other logic operations can be achieved.

So in effect any logic operations can be implemented on a chip with the correct number of 'basic inverters'.

In practice all logic operations can be implemented in this way from any of the different gates. The operation chosen as the basic unit will be the one that results in the cheapest and easiest way to make gates. This depends on the manufacturing technology or type of logic used (DTL, TTL, CMOS, etc). In CMOS, for instance, the basic building block is the inverter. Two inverters in series cancel logically and make a buffer.

If the output of a NAND gate, itself made from inverters, is inverted the result is an AND operation.

If the output of a NOR gate, itself made from inverters, is inverted the result is an OR operation.

Before the days of LSI, and microprocessors on one chip, complicated logic circuits had to be built up from lots of smaller chips. These are still used to provide support circuits for microprocessors. Each chip might contain about four or six identical circuits. For instance four NAND gates, four OR gates, six buffers etc. One such set of chips is the 7400 series (e.g. 7400, 7401, 7402, etc.) implemented in TTL and others are the 4000 and 74C series implemented in CMOS.

The cheapest gates to manufacture, and hence the most inexpensive to buy, are NAND gates and inverters. It is therefore common when building up chips into larger circuits to have a supply of NAND gates and use only these to produce any other functions required. In this way it is also often possible to use up spare gates on one chip in other parts of the circuit.

A NAND with its inputs joined gives a NOT. An AND is given by inverting the output of a NAND.

An OR is given by inverting the inputs to a NAND, and a NOR is given by inverting this.

To see if you really do understand logic operations it would be a good idea to check these and the previous CMOS combinations out to see if they work.

How do I check out logic implementations?

You do this by drawing up a truth table. Let's look at an OR operation made from two NOTS and a NAND shown in Fig. 4.7. When both inputs are zero the output is zero because the inverters change the original 0s input into V+ inputs to the NAND gate.

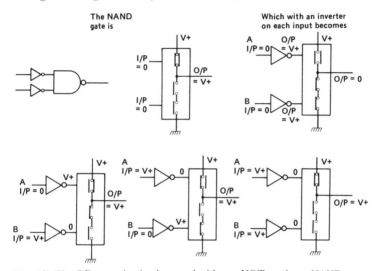

Fig. 4.7. The OR operation implemented with two NOTs and one NAND gate

If either A or B go to V+, individually or both together, the appropriate input to the NAND gate goes to zero and so the output goes to V+. The truth table for this is:

A	B	output
0	0	0
0	1	1
1	0	1
1	1	1

which is an OR operation.

Now try some of the others yourself.

I thought the switches in microprocessors were transistors. How are real logic gates made?

Yes, they are transistors, and in metal oxide semiconductor chips they are either PMOS, NMOS, or both together, CMOS. It is easy to change our simple 'switch models' of logic operations into real transistor CMOS gate circuits (CMOS, remember, means we use pairs of P-type and N-type MOSFETs).

Fig. 4.8 shows a NOT gate which you have met before.

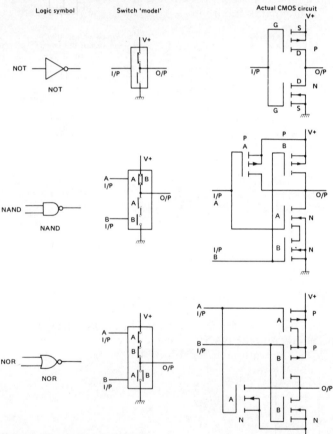

Fig. 4.8. The gates as real circuits

You should be able to identify the two transistors that act as switches. Remember that the gates are connected together so when one transistor is ON the other must be OFF. For example, when the gates are connected to V+ the N channel FET is ON and the P channel FET is OFF so the output is connected to zero.

When the gates are connected to ground the N channel FET is OFF and the P channel FET is ON so the output is connected to V+.

This is the basic CMOS circuit and such complementary pairs of FETs will be seen repeated over and over again in more complicated CMOS circuits.

Now look at the NAND gate in Fig. 4.8. You should again be able to identify the transistors; four this time, one P channel and one N channel for each input.

Get a scrap of paper and work out which are on and which are off for different inputs. Compare your results with the truth table for a NAND gate. They should be the same! The NOR gate is just as easy.

Don't forget that an OR gate can be made by putting an inverter (NOT) after a NOR – just two extra transistors. Also an AND can be made by putting an inverter (NOT) after a NAND. A buffer is just two inverters (NOTs) in series.

If you have been looking in CMOS data books you may have noticed that sometimes diodes are included in the circuits. These do not affect the working of the circuit but are there to protect it. The layer of oxide between gate and channel in a MOSFET is very thin and can be damaged by voltages above about 60 volts. These diodes provide an alternative path to try and save the MOSFETs. Even so you should be very careful when handling MOSFET circuits. A static charge on *you* due to a wool/nylon carpet or pullover can ruin a MOSFET device. Don't touch the pins of the chip, if possible work on an earthed surface and discharge yourself to it before you start work!

What about seeing how these gates are used?

They are used all over the microcomputer for logic operations, arithmetic and controlling the flow of data.

Let's look first at one more gate and then we will be able to see very quickly how two numbers can be compared to see if they are the same or not.

The new gate to be introduced is the EXCLUSIVE OR gate (XOR). This is like the OR gate but does not give an output if both inputs are present, (V+), at the same time. In other words it is EXCLUSIVELY one input OR the other but not both together.

The logic symbol for an EXCLUSIVE OR gate is shown in Fig. 4.9.

In CMOS it can be thought of as three inverters shown as 'switch models' in Fig. 4.9.

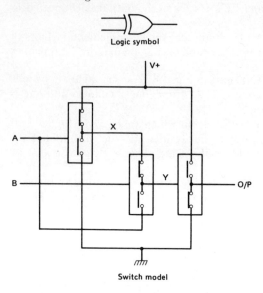

Logic symbol

Switch model

Fig. 4.9. The EXCLUSIVE OR gate

When $A = 0$ and $B = 0$ then $X = \bar{A} = V+$, $Y = X = V+$, and therefore output $= 0$.

When $A = V+$ and $B = 0$ then $X = \bar{A} = 0$, $Y = X = 0$, and therefore output $= V+$.

When $A = 0$ and $B = V+$ then $X = V+$, but $Y = A = 0$, and therefore output $= V+$.

When $A = V+$ and $B = V+$ then $X = 0$, but $Y = A = V+$, and therefore output $= 0$.

The truth table for this operation is:

A	B	A XOR B
0	0	0
0	1	1
1	0	1
1	1	0

and EXCLUSIVE OR is written as ⊕. So A ⊕ B means the A EXCLUSIVE OR B operation.

44

Now if we NOT the EXCLUSIVE OR gate we get the following truth table:

A	B	Output
0	0	1
0	1	0
1	0	0
1	1	1

Notice that the output is V+ only if the two inputs are the same. We can compare two numbers! This circuit is called a comparator. The operation is called a COINCIDENCE operation and is written as $\odot$. A $\odot$ B means the A COINCIDENCE B operation. In order to compare one eight-bit binary number with another, eight such circuits are required, one for each data line.

5
Arithmetic

How does the microprocessor perform arithmetic?

Before we look at the circuits required let's see how we add in binary arithmetic. Look at the binary numbers for decimal 0 to 15 again.

Decimal	Binary
0	0000
1	0001
2	0010
3	0011
4	0100
5	0101
6	0110
7	0111
8	1000
9	1001
10	1010
11	1011
12	1100
13	1101
14	1110
15	1111

Let's add binary 0001 to binary 0101

```
  0101        In the RH (least significant digit)
+ 0001        column 1 + 1 = 0 and carry 1
  ----
    0
    1
(carry 1)
```

```
  0101        In the second column 0 + 0 + the
+ 0001        (carry 1) = 1
  ----
   10
```

```
  0101         In the third column 1 + 0 = 1 no carry
+ 0001         to add. So enter 1 in the answer
  ────
   110

  0101         In the fourth column 0 + 0 = 0 no carry
+ 0001         to add so enter 0 in the answer
  ────
  0110
```

You can check this result from the table:

```
0101 = decimal 5
0001 = decimal 1.
```

Decimal 5 + decimal 1 = decimal 6 which from the table is 0110 in binary. The answer we got! Try adding binary 0001 to a few more numbers yourself.

To save writing the words decimal and binary all the time the base of the system we are using, 16 for hex, 10 for decimal and 2 for binary, is written in small print after the number. Sometimes an H is used instead of 16 in hex. So decimal 6 is written as 6_{10}, binary 0110 as 0110_2. Hexadecimal OF would be written as OF_{16} or OFH.

Now for the complicated stuff!

Add 0110_2 to 0011_2

```
  0110₂
+ 0011₂
```

The answer is 1001_2

Now try
```
  0111₂
+ 0011₂
```

The first column is easy; $1_2 + 1_2 = 0_2$ carry 1_2. The next column is more difficult until you get used to it; $1_2 + 1_2$ plus the carried 1_2.

We know $0001_2 + 0001_2 + 0001_2$ is $1_{10} + 1_{10} + 1_{10} = 3_{10}$ in decimal, but this is 11_2 in binary. What we do is write 1_2 in the answer and carry 1_2 just like you would in decimal. The final answer is 1010_2.

You have now carried out every possible operation required for the addition of two binary integers (whole numbers). There are eight possible alternatives and if we want to design a circuit to carry them out we need to draw up a truth table.

The eight alternatives that occur when we add one binary number A to another binary number B are:

$$A = 0 \qquad\qquad\qquad = 0$$
$$+ B = \underline{0} \qquad\qquad\qquad + \underline{0}$$

        (no carry in)   0   = result or sum and no carry over

$$A = 0 \qquad\qquad\qquad = 0$$
$$+ B = \underline{0} \qquad\qquad\qquad + \underline{0}$$

                              1_2 = result and no carry over

    1_2 (carry in 1_2)

$$A = 0 \qquad\qquad\qquad = 0$$
$$+ B = \underline{1_2} \qquad\qquad\qquad + \underline{1_2}$$

        (no carry in) 1_2 and no carry over

$$A = 0 \qquad\qquad\qquad = 0$$
$$+ B = \underline{1_2} \qquad\qquad\qquad + 1_2$$

                          and carry over 1_2

    1_2 (carry in 1_2) 1_2 (carry in 1_2)

$$A = 1_2 \qquad\qquad\qquad = 1_2$$
$$+ B = \underline{0} \qquad\qquad\qquad + \underline{0}$$

        (no carry in) 1_2 and no carry over

$$A = 1_2 \qquad\qquad\qquad = 1_2$$
$$+ B = \underline{0} \qquad\qquad\qquad + 0$$

                         0   and carry over 1_2

    1_2 (carry in 1_2) 1_2

$$A = 1_2 \qquad\qquad\qquad = 1_2$$
$$+ B = \underline{1_2} \qquad\qquad\qquad + 1_2$$

        (no carry in)   0   and carry over 1_2

                       1_2

$$A = 1_2 \qquad\qquad\qquad = 1_2$$
$$+ B = \underline{1_2} \qquad\qquad\qquad + 1_2$$

                       1_2 and carry over 1_2

    1_2 (carry in 1_2) 1_2

Each of these possibilities can be expressed in the form of a truth table with one line for each possibility.

INPUT			OUTPUT	
Ai	Bi	Carry in (Ci)	Result of Sum (S)	Carry over (C)
0	0	0	0	0
0	0	1	1	0
0	1	0	1	0
0	1	1	0	1
1	0	0	1	0
1	0	1	0	1
1	1	0	0	1
1	1	1	1	1

Can this truth table be implemented using a combination of gates?

Yes, a circuit known as a full adder does this. The whole full adder though will only add one binary digit to one other, along with any carry in digit. In order to add one eight-bit data word to another you require eight full adders connected together in parallel.

In a microcomputer two eight-bit numbers can be added together by obtaining the augend $(A_7A_6A_5A_4A_3A_2A_1A_0)$ from the accumulator register and the addend $(B_7B_6B_5B_4B_3B_2B_1B_0)$ from memory, or perhaps another register, and adding them in an adder circuit. (Addend = number to be added; augend = number to which the addend is to be added.) The result or sum $S_7S_6S_5S_4S_3S_2S_1S_0$ is then usually transferred to the accumulator where it erases the previous contents and is ready for any further successive additions, or for transfer elsewhere.

A full adder has to be capable of accepting three inputs, A, B and any carry in. It is actually made from two half adders with their carry outs OR'ed together.

A half adder accepts only two inputs and gives two outputs. It is easy to implement. A half adder cannot add in a carry, because it has only two inputs, so two half adders have to be used together to make a full adder. This will then add two inputs A and B and a carry in. It will give two outputs: the result or sum, S, and a carry out, C.

The truth table for a half adder is:

A	B	C	S
0	0	0	0
0	1	0	0
1	0	0	1
1	1	1	0

e.g. line 1 $A = 0$
   + $B = 0$
      $S = 0$ carry 0

line 2 $A = 0$
   + $B = 1$
      $S = 1$ carry 0

line 3 $A = 1$
   + $B = 0$
      $S = 1$ carry 0

line 4 $A = 1$
   + $B = 1$
      $S = 0$ carry 1

The logic implementation of a half adder is shown in Fig. 5.1 and requires only two gates, an EXCLUSIVE OR and an AND. Try drawing up the truth table for these gates to check that it *is* a half adder:

A	B	C	S
0	0		
0	1		
1	0		
1	1		

Use the truth tables for AND and EXCLUSIVE OR to help work it out.

AND

A	B	output (C)
0	0	0
0	1	0
1	0	0
1	1	1

EXCLUSIVE OR

A	B	output (S)
0	0	0
0	1	1
1	0	1
1	1	0

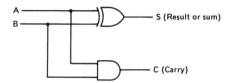

Fig. 5.1. The half adder

Check back to make sure you got it right.

If you didn't, the way you would work it out is:

if A = B = 0 the output of the exclusive OR (which is S) is 0 and the output of the AND (which is C) is 0.

Next move to the second line of each table:

A = 0, B = 1, therefore C from the AND table is 0 and S from the EXCLUSIVE OR table is 1, and so on.

In CMOS it is easier to make a NAND gate then NOT it to give the AND function so you will come across the half adder implemented in that way or implemented entirely in NAND gates and inverters.

What is a full adder?

A full adder is shown in Fig. 5.2 and is made from two half adders connected together. In order to produce a truth table for this circuit you will need to refer to the truth tables for XOR, AND and OR gates:

EXCLUSIVE OR			AND			OR		
A	B	output S_1 or S_2	A	B	output C_1 or C_2	A	B	output
0	0	0	0	0	0	0	0	0
0	1	1	0	1	0	0	1	1
1	0	1	1	0	0	1	0	1
0	0	0	1	1	1	1	1	1

The first line is given by A = 0, B = 0, carry in = 0. The output of the left EXCLUSIVE OR gate (S_1) is 0 from the above table. This is input, along with the carry in of 0, to the second EXCLUSIVE OR gate and its output is found from the table to be 0. This is the sum out S.

51

The output C_1 from the left AND gate is zero and this is input to the OR gate, along with the output of the second AND gate C_2, which in this case is

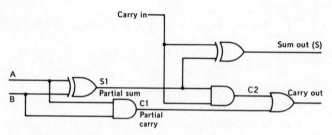

Fig. 5.2. The full adder

also zero (because its inputs are both 0). The carry out is therefore zero. You can complete the rest of the truth table for a full adder in the same way.

Full adder truth table

A	B	Carry in	Partial Carry C_1	Partial Sum_1	Partial Carry C_2	Sum S	Carry out Co
0	0	0	0	0	0	0	0
0	0	1					
0	1	0					
0	1	1					
1	0	0					
1	0	1					
1	1	0					
1	1	1					

The next line with inputs $A = 0$, $B = 0$, carry in $= 1$, is $C_1 = 0$, $S_1 = 0$, $C_2 = 0$, $S = 1$, $C_0 = 0$. Either work the rest out or copy them in from the table for the eight possible addition combinations.

How is eight-bit arithmetic carried out?

The full adder will add together two binary digits and a carry in. We need eight for an eight-bit word and must connect the carry out from the least significant bit to the carry in of the next and so on along the line. The final carry out can go to a special part of the micro-processor known as a flag to let us know that there is a carry out from the adder.

This is useful for 16-bit, or more, arithmetic which is carried out eight bits at a time. A carry out from the end of the eight-bit register means that we end up with a number greater than $1111\ 1111_2$ in it.

What are an Add With Carry instruction and a plain Add instruction?

The add with carry (ADC) instruction that we looked at for a 'typical microprocessor' would include the placing of any carry out, the binary digit 1, in a one-bit store called a carry flag. The full add with carry instruction would now be: add the contents of the memory address I specify directly after this op-code to the contents of the accumulator, also add any carry in from the carry flag. Put the answer back in the accumulator instead of the number that is already there. If there is a final carry out from this addition place it in the carry flag store. (Set the carry flag.)

The add 'without carry' (ADD) instruction previously mentioned, although not adding a carry in to the addition, would store any carry out in the carry flag ready for future use, if required, by an add with carry instruction.

What is meant by a 'look ahead' adder?

A simple adder circuit of full adders connected for parallel addition (eight bits side by side) is called a ripple adder and does not give an instant answer as you might expect because each carry out has to travel, or ripple, through all eight stages in turn in a serial fashion. This can cause significant delays in obtaining the final result.

A faster adder can be made that effectively generates the carries for all digit positions at once and cuts down the delay time. This is known as a 'look ahead' carry adder.

How is 16-bit arithmetic carried out?

Sixteen-bit numbers can be added in two eight-bit chunks by first adding the least significant (right-hand) eight digits of each number, storing any carry over (which can only be a 0 or a 1) in a one-bit register in the MPU called a carry flag, and then adding this in to the next eight bits.

The sequence would be:

1. Read the first eight bits of each number from memory. Add these numbers together using the ADD instruction. Store the result back in memory and put any carry into the carry flag register.
2. Read the next eight bits of each number from memory and add them along with the contents of the carry flag register using the ADC instruction. Store the final result in the memory.

Example:
$$00010010 \quad 11111011_2$$
$$+ \; 01101000 \quad 10000001_2$$
$$\overline{01111011 \quad 01111100_2}$$

would be carried out as:

$$11111011_2$$
$$10000001_2$$
$$\overline{01111100_2}$$

with carry one entered in carry flag;

then:
$$00010010_2$$
$$01101000_2$$
$$\underline{\qquad 1_2 \qquad} \text{(from carry flag)}$$
$$01111011_2$$

Any carry this time would be due to an overflow error, i.e. a number greater than $11111111 \; 11111111$ in total.

An overflow would already have occurred, though, once $01111111 \; 11111111$ had been exceeded. This will be explained more fully later. It is because the left-hand digit can be used to indicate whether the number is positive or negative and it is called the sign bit. 0 is used to indicate a positive number and 1 to indicate a negative number.

What about subtraction?

Look at this addition first:

$$1111 \quad 1111_2$$
$$+ \; 0000 \quad 0001_2$$
$$\overline{0000 \quad 0000} \qquad \text{and carry 1, but don't worry about this yet.}$$

$0000\ 0001_2$ is binary for decimal 1_{10}. We have to add -1_{10} to $+1_{10}$ in order to get zero $(-1_{10}+1_{10}=0)$.

Therefore the binary number $1111\ 1111_2$ can be used to represent -1_{10} because when we add it to $+0000\ 0001_2$ which is $+1_{10}$ we get $0000\ 0000_2$ ($A-B$ is the same as $A+(-B)$).

If $1111\ 1111_2$ represents -1_{10} what represents -2_{10}? Well this must be one less than -1_{10} so, in binary, one less than $1111\ 1111_2$ is $1111\ 1110_2$ and this represents -2_{10}. -3_{10} is $1111\ 1101_2$ and so on.

Decimal	Binary	Decimal	Binary
+ 15	0000 1111	− 1	1111 1111
+ 14	0000 1110	− 2	1111 1110
+ 13	0000 1101	− 3	1111 1101
+ 12	0000 1100	− 4	1111 1100
+ 11	0000 1011	− 5	1111 1011
+ 10	0000 1010	− 6	1111 1010
+ 9	0000 1001	− 7	1111 1001
+ 8	0000 1000	− 8	1111 1000
+ 7	0000 0111	− 9	1111 0111
+ 6	0000 0110	−10	1111 0110
+ 5	0000 0101	−11	1111 0101
+ 4	0000 0100	−12	1111 0100
+ 3	0000 0011	−13	1111 0011
+ 2	0000 0010	−14	1111 0010
+ 1	0000 0001	−15	1111 0001
0	0000 0000		

This type of representation of positive and negative numbers is known as 2s complement representation.

The positive numbers remain the same but the negative number representation can be obtained by complementing the positive number (passing it through inverter gates would do this, but later you will see this is not necessary because the accumulator register can easily create the complement of the number it stores), and then adding 1 in an adder circuit.

For instance 1_{10} = $0000\ 0001_2$ in binary
Complemented, this is $1111\ 1110_2$
which, when 1 is added $1111\ 1110$
  $+1$
  _____
becomes $=1111\ 1111_2$

This is -1_{10} in 2s complement form.

Try -13_{10} for yourself and check your answer in the last table.

Let's try a few more subtractions in the form $A - B$ is $A + (-B)$. Try $5_{10} - 2_{10}$ or $5_{10} + (-2_{10}) = 3_{10}$.

5_{10} is	$0000\ 0101_2$ (minuend)
-2_{10} in 2s comp is	$1111\ 1110_2$ (2s complement of subtrahend)
added gives	$0000\ 0011_2$ (difference)

and carry one, but ignore this for now. It is not a true overflow as the rest of the number is not $1111\ 1111_2$. $0000\ 0011_2$ is found from the table to be 3_{10}, the correct answer.

Now try $3_{10} - 5_{10}$ or $3_{10} + (-5_{10}) = -2_{10}$.

3_{10} is	$0000\ 0011_2$ (minuend)
-5_{10} in 2s comp is	$1111\ 1011_2$ (2s complement of subtrahend)
	$1111\ 1110_2$ (difference)

with no carry.
$1111\ 1110_2$ is found from our table to be -2_{10}, the correct answer.

If you are really into this maths then try

$-3_{10} + (-5_{10})$ *to see how this comes out (i.e. the addition of two negative numbers).*

$-3_{10} + (-5_{10}) = -8_{10}$

-3_{10} *in 2s comp. is*	$1111\ 1101_2$
-5_{10} *in 2s comp. is*	$1111\ 1011_2$
	$1111\ 1000_2$

and carry one.
$1111\ 1000_2$ *is found from our table to be* -8_{10}*, the correct answer.*

What about carries at the left though? Well, if you invert them you get $\bar{C}$ (Not carry). It might help you to think of $\bar{C}$ as a borrow. We implement subtraction by addition of the 2s complement, so the carry in the addition of 2s complement serves the same purpose as a borrow in normal subtraction. The carry out at the end of an eight-bit number can be used to enable us to subtract two 16-bit numbers with an eight-bit adder in the same way as we add them. All we have to do is store the carry in a one-bit flag register after adding the lowest eight digits then add the carry in to the addition of the next eight digits.

For example:

$$01100001\ 10001001_2 \quad \text{minuend}$$
$$\text{minus} \quad 01000001\ 00010001_2 \quad \text{subtrahend}$$

First find the 2s complement of $01000001\ 00010001_2$

| inverted = | $10111110\ 11101110_2$ |
| | $+1$ |

2s complement = $\quad 10111110\ 11101111_2$

Therefore $\quad\quad 01100001\ 10001001_2$
$\quad\quad\quad\quad + 10111110\ 11101111_2$

$\quad\quad\quad\quad 00100000\ 01111000_2$

carry 1 $\quad\quad\quad$ carry 1

This is the answer and the final carry just indicates that the sign of the answer is the same as the sign of the minuend. (I.e. $\bar{C} = 0$. There was no borrow because the minuend was greater than the subtrahend.)

If at the end of each calculation there is no carry out ($C = 0$) then $\bar{C} = 1$, i.e. there had to be a final borrow. This simply means that the subtrahend was greater than the minuend.

The last 16-bit subtraction could be done in two parts with an eight-bit adder: first the eight least significant digits of each number:

$$10001001_2$$
$$11101111_2$$
$$01111000_2$$

and carry one (i.e. set the carry flag).

This answer is returned to memory and the next half of the calculation carried out with the carry in added in.

$$01100001_2$$
$$10111110_2$$
$$\quad\quad\ 1_2 \text{ carry in}$$
$$00100000_2 \quad \text{and carry 1.}$$

This half of the answer is then also returned to memory.

57

What is the sign bit?

We have to have some way of knowing if we are dealing with a positive or negative number so the most significant digit (the one on the left) is used for this purpose. It is set at 0 for a positive number and 1 for a negative number and is called the sign bit. The rest of the number is known as its magnitude.

This means that two eight-bit words can have 15 bits representing the magnitude of the number and one bit as its sign. So we can handle whole numbers from 0111111111111111_2 which is $+32\,767_{10}$ to $1\,000000000000000_2$ which is $-32\,768_{10}$.

One eight-bit word, with the most significant bit used as the sign bit, could handle whole numbers from 01111111_2 which is $+127_{10}$ to 10000000_2 which is -128_{10}.

If we try to add two large positive numbers together that give a result greater than 01111111_2 in the eight most significant bits then the registers cannot cope:

$$
\begin{array}{rcl}
0\ 1111100_2 &=& 124_{10} \\
0\ 1100111_2 &=& 103_{10} \\
\hline
1\ 1100011_2 &\neq& 227_{10}
\end{array}
$$

sign bit   magnitude

The answer is wrong due to an overflow error. *What has actually happened is that after the addition of 3 the register has reached the largest number possible with seven magnitude bits 01111111 (i.e. $+127_{10}$). There is still $(103-3)=100$ left to add. The next 1 sets the register to 10000000 which is -128 and there is still $(100-1)=99$ left to add which takes us to $(-128+99)=-29$ which is the answer shown, 1100011_2 in magnitude.*

Whenever a true overflow error occurs as in this example the sign bit in the answer is automatically different from the sign bits of the numbers being added, which will have to be the same sign as each other if they are going to cause an overflow when added together.

Similarly when adding two large negative numbers:

$$
\begin{array}{rcl}
1\ 0000001_2 &=& -127_{10} \\
+1\ 0000011_2 &=& -125_{10} \\
\hline
0\ 0000100_2 &\neq& -252_{10}
\end{array}
$$

This condition of the reversal of sign bits can be tested for and used to set a one-bit overflow flag register to indicate that something has gone wrong.

One-bit flag registers such as the carry and overflow registers are often grouped together for convenience in a part of the MPU called the status, or flag, register.

All arithmetic and logic takes place in a part of the microprocessor called the arithmetic and logic unit. Think of this as being rather like an eight-bit adder, but you can change the actual operations it carries out by putting instruction signals into it.

Most arithmetic and logic units in microprocessors have an instruction to subtract, which causes the data in the accumulator to be complemented, one to be added to it and then this to be summed with the contents of a specified memory location and the final answer to be put back in the accumulator.

If there is not a single instruction to cover all this there will be several separate instructions that will allow you to do it one step at a time.

What about multiplication and division?

These are not usually provided in a microprocessor as operations and have to be achieved by the 'pencil and paper method' explained later. These are then carried out by a program subroutine (part of a program).

Before you will be able to understand how multiplication, division, fractions and extra large numbers are handled by the arithmetic and logic unit we will have to look at the accumulator register in detail because this is so closely linked with the arithmetic and logic unit that an understanding of it is essential before the complete working of the ALU can be described. However we must first look at registers in general.

6
Registers

What are registers?

Registers are temporary stores inside the MPU, some having dedicated tasks and some for more general use. The accumulator is a general purpose register that is closely connected with the arithmetic and logic unit. Most of the data manipulation takes place using the accumulator.

What is meant by combinational and sequential logic?

All the gates that we have looked at so far have been combinational logic, which means that the output depends only on the present inputs. The output appears immediately the inputs are connected (except for any slight propagation delay). Registers can be constructed in such a way that their logic is sequential, which means their present output can depend on a sequence of previous events. This is what makes them particularly useful as temporary stores and for the manipulation of data.

How are registers implemented?

Registers are made up of a series of circuits known as flip-flops, one flip-flop for each bit of the register. Flip-flops are circuits that have two stable states: either ON to signify a 1 or OFF to signify a 0. So a typical sequence might start with output = 0 and input = 0. Then the input goes to V+ and so does the output. The input goes back to zero but the output stays at V+. It might then require a different sequence of events to set it back to zero again.

Some registers have to allow for two-way flow of data and some have to allow for data to be fed in in serial form (one bit at a time) and out in parallel (eight bits at a time) or vice versa.

This type of register is then acting as an input or output port on the end of the data lines and can be used to interface the micro-computer to a serial peripheral, such as a tape recorder, VDU, etc.

What is a flip-flop and what does it do when it flips?

You can imagine the flip-flop to be replaced by ganged switches between the output and the supply voltage $V+$ or ground 0 V. The switches can only take up the two positions shown in Fig. 6.1.

The output can therefore have only two possible values, 0 or $V+$, and will remain stable in either position once set. It can therefore be used to store a binary digit. An output of $V+$ represents binary 1 in store and an output of zero represents binary 0.

It should be fairly obvious that the actual output is supplied by a 'basic inverter' unit and that there must also be other circuitry in the box with it to latch the output into either of its stable states (hatched area of Fig. 6.1). We shall come back to this circuitry later. Before we can understand it we need to examine the various inputs to the flip-flop.

Look at the S-R flip-flop in Fig. 6.1. Assume the output state is unknown, i.e. either 0 or 1. There is a reset (R) or clear input. When this is connected to $V+$ the flip-flop output goes to zero if it was $V+$, but stays at zero if it was already zero. This remains even if R returns to 0. Further connection of R to $V+$ has no effect until after the flip-flop has been set again. This is done with another similar input called a SET input. A $V+$ voltage state present at the set input causes the switches to change the output back to $V+$ again.

The flip-flop remains in this stable state no matter what subsequently happens to the S input until the reset input is taken to $V+$ again, whereupon the circuit resets to output 0.

This type of flip-flop is known as an S-R (set-reset) flip-flop.

There are also clocked S-R flip-flops in which a clock pulse must also be present at the same time as either the S or the R input in order for the flip-flop to flip.

The S-R flip-flop works fine if the inputs are only allowed to take up opposite states but if they are both connected to $V+$ at the same time the output is unpredictable.

This is overcome in the D-type flip-flop which has only one input that sets or resets the flip-flop automatically, i.e. an input of $V+$ sets it and an input of zero resets it. The clocked D-type flip-flop also has an 'enable', or clock, input as well as a single data input. The data input, either $V+$ or 0, is transferred to the output only when a $V+$ clock signal is also present.

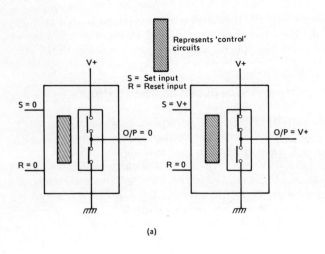

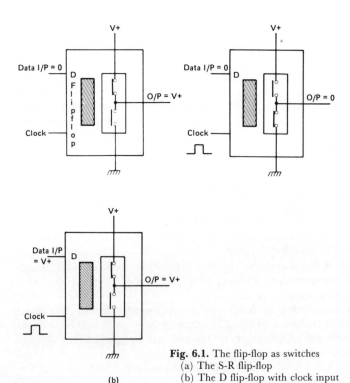

Fig. 6.1. The flip-flop as switches
(a) The S-R flip-flop
(b) The D flip-flop with clock input

A typical sequence of events could be:
1. The D-type flip-flop output is already at V+.
2. A voltage of zero at the data input at the arrival of a V+ clock pulse will reset the output to zero, but a voltage of V+ at the data input at the arrival of the clock pulse would leave the output set at V+.

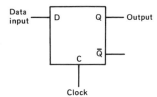

Data input — D Q — Output

C Q̄

Clock

Fig. 6.2. The D-type flip-flop

A data input without a clock pulse present has no effect on the output.

The logic symbol for a D-type flip-flop is shown in Fig. 6.2.

How are binary numbers stored?

Eight flip-flops can be used together to store eight-bit binary numbers. There are actually two sets of 'switches' per flip-flop and so in practice there can be two outputs, one of which, $\bar{Q}$, will always be the opposite or complement of the other, Q.

How do we load numbers into and out of registers?

This can be done all eight bits at a time in parallel and also one bit at a time in serial form.

In parallel should be fairly obvious. If each data line from the data bus is connected to the input of a separate D-type flip-flop then as soon as their clock inputs are taken to V+ they will store the data present on the data bus and will continue to do so until the next clock pulse arrives, at which point their outputs will change to the new data present on the data lines.

For serial input the register is much the same but the output from one flip-flop has to be connected to the input of the next. Data is then fed one bit at a time, in synchronisation with the clock pulses, to the first flip-flop. This passes each bit on to the next flip-flop, and so on down the line.

It isn't quite as simple as it appears because if that was all we did it would be possible for each bit to be transferred immediately through all the stages and we would end up eventually with either 0000 0000 or 1111 1111 stored depending on the value of the last bit in.

Either a type of flip-flop known as an edge-triggered flip-flop, or another type known as a master-slave flip-flop, can be used to overcome this 'domino effect'. These also overcome timing problems that can arise, for instance if the flip-flop switching time is faster than the clock pulse.

Think of a master-slave flip-flop as being like two flip-flops cascaded together in the same box. They are arranged so that on arrival of the clock pulse the first flip-flop is enabled and the second disabled. So the output of the first flip-flop becomes the same as its data input. When the clock pulse is removed the second flip-flop is enabled and the first disabled, so the output of the first is transferred to the output of the second. In this way a delay is introduced and the 'domino effect' is avoided.

You will also come across a J-K flip-flop. This has two outputs, Q and $\bar{Q}$, and two inputs, J and K, and possibly a clock input as well. It is similar to the S-R flip-flop but inputs of $J = K = 1$ are this time allowed. J is like the set input and K is like the reset input.

Master-slave J-K flip-flops can be connected together to form a serial input register as shown in Fig. 6.3.

A single data input is often provided to the first stage for serial input and is sometimes referred to as a $J-\bar{K}$ input because it is achieved by connecting K to J via a NOT gate. D-type master-slave flip-flops can also be used to make a serial register.

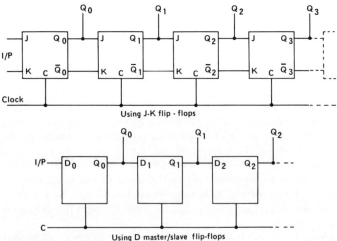

Fig. 6.3. Serial registers

64

In addition to the inputs already mentioned many registers also have an all-clear input that will reset every flip-flop to zero output regardless of the clock pulse. Sometimes an all-set input (preset) is also provided.

Some registers also have shift/load controls. This can allow flip-flops to be loaded in parallel and then read out in serial form (shifted) and vice versa.

How are these flip-flops built up from our basic inverter switch?

Let's look at the simple S-R flip-flop first.

Imagine two inverters connected in a closed loop with the input to the first called S and its output $\bar{Q}$, and the input to the second called R and its output Q. See Fig. 6.4.

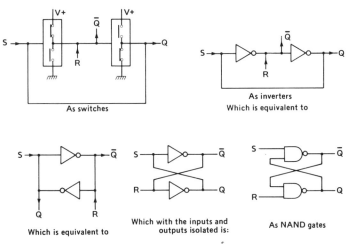

Fig. 6.4. The S-R flip-flop

If Q is zero then the input to the first inverter switch is zero so its output is V+ and this is input to the second inverter switch and holds its output at zero. This is a stable condition.

$$S = 0 \qquad Q = 0$$
$$R = V+ \qquad Q = V+$$

If S is now set to V+ the first inverter switches and its output goes to zero. This is input to the second inverter, which also switches, and its output goes to V+ which is fed back to S to maintain this stable

65

state even when the original input is removed. So this circuit can be set to $V+$ by an input at S. In the same way it can be reset to zero by an input to R. It is an S-R (set-reset) flip-flop.

Just as we drew up truth tables for our combinational logic functions so we can draw up truth tables, sometimes called action tables, for our sequential logic flip-flops. The only difference is that, because the logic is sequential, the next output depends on the present output as well as the inputs. The truth table therefore takes into account present Q, S and R in order to predict Q next.

present Q	S	R	Q next	
0	0	0	0	} Normal 'at rest'
1	0	0	1	} condition
0	1	0	1	} an input at S
1	1	0	1	} sets Q to 1
0	0	1	0	} an input at R
1	0	1	0	} resets Q to zero
0	1	1	unpredictable	
1	1	1		

1 represents $V+$ and 0 represents zero volts. Note that $S = R = 1$ is unpredictable as it can lead to either stable state $Q = 1$, $\bar{Q} = 0$ or $Q = 0$, $\bar{Q} = 1$. In use this condition is often excluded by the use of a single input implemented with a NOT gate between S and R as in the D-type flip-flop.

Sometimes we require a flip-flop that works like the S-R flip-flop but allows the input $R = S = 1$. This type of flip-flop is the J-K flip-flop. An input of $J = K = 1$ causes the output to change state.

If the J and K inputs are connected directly together we obtain a flip-flop that will toggle (change its state) whenever the input is set to $V+$. This type of flip-flop may also have a clock input. It is known as a T flip-flop.

How is it possible to alter the connections to the flip-flops in registers so that they can be read into, and out of, in either serial or parallel?

This is done with gates between the flip-flops in the register. The gates set up different paths for the data depending on what control signals are applied to them.

66

The logic AND operation can be used to set up different paths for signals. An AND gate can be opened by a control signal on one of its inputs and is closed when the control signal is removed.

The circuit shown in Fig. 6.5 will switch either input 1, 2, or 3 to output 1 depending on the control signals C_0, C_1, C_2, C_3 and at the same time either switch the clock to output 2 or not.

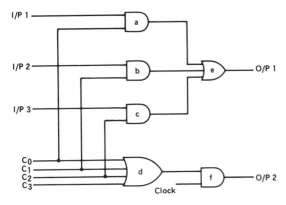

Fig. 6.5. A control circuit

Let's see how it works. If $C_0 = C_1 = C_2 = C_3 = 0$ then the inputs to gate d will be zero. Therefore one input to gate f will be zero and its output is always zero no matter what the value of the clock pulse. If any of C_0, C_1, C_2, or C_3 is set to 1 instead of 0 then the clock pulse will pass through gate f to output 2. When $C_0 = C_1 = C_2 = C_3 = 0$ gates a, b and c also have one input at zero so their outputs are zero, and output 1 is also zero.

If now the control signals are 0001, i.e. $C_0 = 1$, $C_1 = C_2 = C_3 = 0$, then the output of gate a is equal to input 1 and this will pass through gate e to output 1. Gates b and c still have one input at 0 so their outputs are 0.

Similarly when the control input is 0010, i.e. $C_0 = 0$, $C_1 = 1$, $C_2 = C_3 = 0$ then input 2 is connected to output 1 and the clock to output 2.

When the control input is 0100 then input 3 is connected to output 1 and the clock to output 2.

If the control input is 1000 then output 1 is set at zero and the clock pulse is passed to output 2.

If the control signals are stored in flip-flops then we already have $\bar{C}_0$, $\bar{C}_1$, $\bar{C}_2$ and $\bar{C}_3$, generated as well as C_0, C_1, C_2, C_3 and the same logic function can be achieved using only a few 'basic inverters'.

Let us, however, continue to show the AND and OR logic implementations as these enable a more 'logical' understanding of the actual functioning of the circuits.

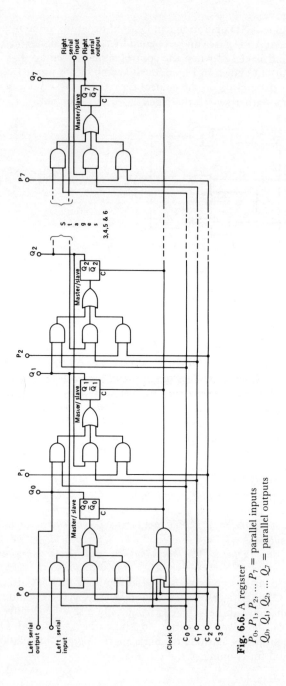

Fig. 6.6. A register
P_0, P_1, P_2, ... P_7 = parallel inputs
Q_0, Q_1, Q_2, ... Q_7 = parallel outputs

68

Now let's see how it is possible to use this type of circuit between flip-flops of the single input/master-slave type to produce a register that can be read into, or out of, in either serial or parallel form. To save space just four flip-flops (Q_0, Q_1, Q_2 and Q_7) are shown in Fig. 6.6.

If the control input is 0001 (see Fig. 6.7) the circuit functions as a shift register and bits fed in one at a time at the left serial input, in synchronisation with the clock pulses, are shifted along the register to the right. Data can be read out either in parallel form, from Q_0, Q_1, Q_2, Q_3, Q_4, Q_5, Q_6, Q_7, or in serial form, from the right output Q_7.

When the control input is 0010 (see Fig. 6.8) then each flip-flop gets its input from the one on its right and bits fed into the right serial input, in synchronisation with the clock pulses, are shifted to

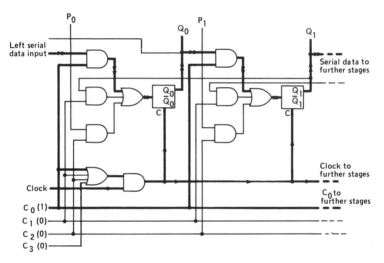

Fig. 6.7

the left along the register. Data can be read out either from the outputs Q_0, Q_1, Q_2, Q_3, Q_4, Q_5, Q_6, Q_7, in parallel form, or in serial form from the left serial output connected to Q_0.

When the control input is 0100 (Fig. 6.9) then each flip-flop reads data from its own parallel input line during the clock pulse, and data can be read out from its parallel output line.

When the control input is 1000 then all the flip-flop inputs are zero so when the next clock pulse arrives all flip-flop outputs will be reset to zero.

69

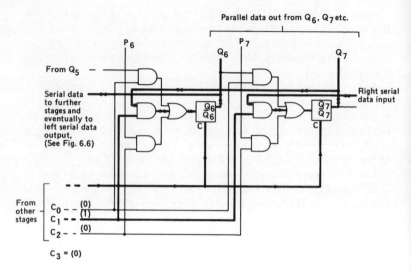

Fig. 6.8

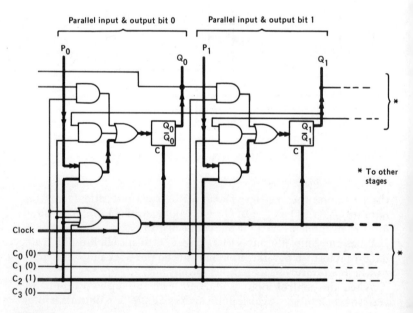

Fig. 6.9

Does the accumulator register have facilities to allow it to shift to the left or right like this?

Yes, it uses shifting to help the arithmetic and logic unit to carry out some of its operations.

How is the accumulator register connected to the arithmetic and logic unit?

It is connected via logic gates which can be controlled by control inputs, just like the shift register's inputs and outputs were controlled. By setting up different paths for the data and routeing it to the appropriate inputs of the flip-flops in a shift register, many different arithmetic and logic operations can be carried out. Such operations as ADD, INCREMENT BY 1, CLEAR, AND, OR, XOR, SHIFT RIGHT, SHIFT LEFT, COMPLEMENT, COMPARE, NEGATIVE CHECK and ZERO CHECK are common. The exact operations provided vary from one microprocessor type to another.

The different inputs from the circuits required for the different operations are 'OR'ed' together at each flip-flop input. Examining all the circuits in detail would be a long job and lead to a very complex circuit. You can get a good understanding of how the arithmetic and logic unit works by examining the circuits required to interconnect it and the accumulator to enable the simple program we developed to CLEAR, LOAD, ADD and STORE to be performed.

The sequence of operations in a typical microprocessor might be: clear the carry flag, store a number $(A_7A_6A_5A_4A_3A_2A_1A_0)$ in the accumulator, store another number $(B_7B_6B_5B_4B_3B_2B_1B_0)$ in a buffer register and then connect this to the adder. Finally, put the sum back in the accumulator in place of the first number. You might then want to carry out further operations on the sum, such as increment by 1, invert or store in memory.

Apart from any rippling through of carries the addition is done in parallel, so we can simplify our circuits by ignoring the shift circuits which we have already explored, and concentrating on one bit of the register (bit i) somewhere in the middle. This is shown in Fig. 6.10. The first and last bits are also shown so that you can see what happens to the carry in and carry out of the whole register. It is convention to call the right hand (least significant digit) of the registers bit 0 and the left hand (most significant digit) bit 7.

Assume that the control inputs (ADD and CLEAR) are 00, and one of the numbers to be added has already been routed to the accumulator inputs and is now stored at its outputs $Q_7Q_6Q_5Q_4Q_3Q_2Q_1Q_0$. The other number has been routed to a buffer register and is stored at its outputs $B_7B_6B_5B_4B_3B_2B_1B_0$. The adder circuit is combinational so it will already be showing the sum at its outputs ($S_7S_6S_5S_4S_3S_2S_1S_0$) and any carries at its carry outputs ($C_7C_6C_5C_4C_3C_2C_1C_0$).

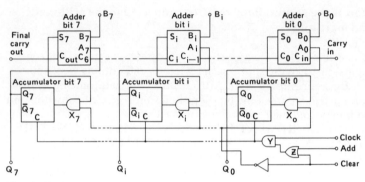

Fig. 6.10. The most significant, the ith, and the least significant bits of the accumulator register

The sum is applied back to the accumulator inputs via AND gates $X_7X_6X_5X_4X_3X_2X_1X_0$. This is because their other inputs are 1 as they are connected to NOT CLEAR ($\overline{\text{Clear}}$) and the control signal clear is zero. This sum does not yet affect the contents of the accumulator because the accumulator is sequential and at the moment no clock pulse can reach it via the AND gate Y. This is because the ADD control and CLEAR control, which are 'OR'ed' together, are both at 0, so one input of AND gate Y is 0 and it cannot give an output. If the ADD control input is set to 1 for the duration of the next clock pulse then the clock pulse is fed to all the accumulator clock inputs via AND gate Y. This causes the sum to be input to the master part of each flip-flop. Then after the clock pulse the sum is transferred automatically from master to slave and appears at the output where it remains if the control inputs are now 00 again. The sum can now be read out in parallel form from the accumulator parallel outputs $Q_7Q_6Q_5Q_4Q_3Q_2Q_1Q_0$ or in serial form using the circuits previously described.

If we wish to CLEAR the accumulator we can do this by making the control inputs 01 for the duration of a clock pulse. This makes the outputs of AND gates $X_7X_6X_5X_4X_3X_2X_1X_0$ zero and therefore ensures that all the accumulator inputs are zero during the clock pulse. Zeros are therefore fed to all the flip-flop outputs when the clock pulse returns to zero. If the accumulator final carry out from bit 7 is connected to the carry flag then this will also be reset to zero by the above operation.

In practice, a separate instruction CLEAR CARRY FLAG is often provided and used to reset the carry flag to zero without affecting the contents of the accumulator.

If we wish to increment the number in the accumulator by 1 we have to have a circuit that will inhibit transfer of any number in the buffer register (or else clear this first). We then allow the number in the accumulator to be fed to the adder and feed a 1 to the first carry in C_0. At the same time we enable the clock pulse to reach all the accumulator flip-flops. The carry in of 1 is therefore added to the number and the sum will be the original number in the accumulator incremented by 1. This will appear in the accumulator after the clock pulse has passed.

The logic shown in Fig. 6.11 will perform this for us.

The AND gates W_0... W_i... W_7 allow the contents of the buffer register to pass to the adder only when the ADD input is 1. When the control inputs are INC = 0, ADD = 1, CLEAR = 0 the number in the buffer register is added

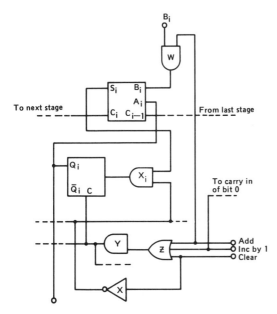

Fig. 6.11. The adder input modified with AND gate W to allow connection of B only when the ADD control signal is 1

73

to the accumulator. When the INC control input is 1 and the ADD control and CLEAR control inputs are both zero then only the accumulator contents and a carry in of 1 are input to the adder. When ADD and INC are both zero, and CLEAR is 1 the accumulator is cleared as before.

So far only single-input flip-flops have been shown to keep the circuitry simple. In practice two-input flip-flops such as J-K flip-flops are used and external gates can connect the inputs as desired to

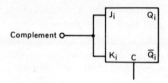

Complement

Fig. 6.12. The J-K flip-flop as a toggle (T) flip-flop

give J-$\bar{\text{K}}$, D, or T, master-slave flip-flops. Connecting the accumulator as T flip-flops and excluding all other inputs to the accumulator is very useful and when V+ (i.e. 1) is applied to each flip-flop input, the number in the accumulator is inverted at the next clock pulse. This is useful for producing the complement of the number ready to increment it later by 1 to obtain the 2s complement for subtraction. (Fig. 6.12).

If we wish to see if the number in the accumulator is negative all we have to do is 'AND' the final output (Q_7) (which will be 1 for a

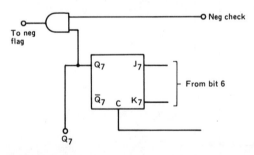

Neg check

To neg flag

From bit 6

Fig. 6.13. Negative check

negative number and 0 for a positive number) with a NEGATIVE CHECK control input of 1. If the output is 1 this can be used to set a one-bit negative flag register, (usually called a sign flag). See Fig. 6.13.

A zero check is similar. All the NOT OUTPUTS $\bar{Q}_0 \bar{Q}_1 \bar{Q}_2 \bar{Q}_3 \bar{Q}_4 \bar{Q}_5 \bar{Q}_6 \bar{Q}_7$ are 'AND'ed with a ZERO CHECK input. Only if all the

74

outputs are zero, i.e. all the NOT OUTPUTS are 1, will the AND gate give an output. This can be used to set a zero flag. (Fig. 6.14).

Logic operations can also be performed by the accumulator. For instance if we wish to LOGIC AND a number in a buffer register

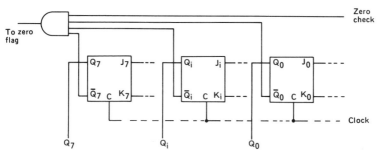

Fig. 6.14. Zero check

with the number in the accumulator this can be achieved by applying NOT B to the accumulator's K inputs.

LOGIC OR can be obtained by applying B to the J inputs of the accumulator and LOGIC EXCLUSIVE OR (XOR) by applying B to the J and K inputs together. If this result is then inverted we have performed a LOGIC COINCIDENCE operation. That is, we have compared two numbers to see if they are the same.

We now know how an arithmetic and logic unit and its accumulator register can ADD, INCREMENT BY 1, CLEAR, SHIFT LEFT, SHIFT RIGHT, COMPLEMENT, COMPARE, perform LOGIC AND, OR, XOR, and check for a NEGATIVE number or for ZERO. These operations also enable us to carry out multiplication and division and to handle floating point arithmetic.

7
Multiplication and division

**How are multiplication and division carried out by the
arithmetic and logic unit?**

Multiplication and division are not usually provided as separate
instructions. When they are though they are carried out by the ALU
in the same way that you would do it with pencil and paper.

Consider the following two binary numbers being multiplied
together:

$$\begin{array}{ll} 00001010 & \text{multiplicand} \\ 00001011 & \text{multiplier} \end{array} \times$$

First the multiplicand is multiplied by the least significant digit
(right hand digit) of the multiplier:

$$\begin{array}{l} 00001010 \\ 00001011 \end{array} \times \quad \text{(to obtain the answer multiply 00001010 by 1)}$$

00001010 = first partial product

We next multiply the multiplicand by the second digit of the
multiplier and place the second partial product one digit to the left
(just as in decimal):

00001011

00001010 = second partial product

We repeat this with each of the multiplier digits in turn and then
add the partial products together:

$$\begin{array}{l} 00001010 \\ 00001011 \end{array}$$

$$\left. \begin{array}{l} 00001010 \\ 0001010 \\ 000000 \\ 01010 \end{array} \right\} \text{partial products}$$

01101110 = final product

The final product must fit in the register and must therefore be less than 01111111 if it is positive.

The sequence of operations described is achieved in the microprocessor by placing the multiplier and multiplicand in separate shift registers. The outputs of the multiplicand's shift register are connected to the inputs of the accumulator. The least significant, right-hand, bit of the multiplier's register is connected to circuitry that can connect it when required to the ADD control of the ALU. The B inputs to the ALU are set to zero. See Fig. 7.1.

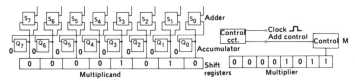

Fig. 7.1

The right-hand digit of the multiplier is then connected to the ADD control of the ALU during the next clock pulse. If the right-hand digit is a 1 then the multiplicand will be added into the accumulator to form the first partial product and will appear at its outputs Q_7 Q_6 Q_5 Q_4 Q_3 Q_2 Q_1 Q_0 when the clock pulse returns to zero, as shown in Fig. 7.2.

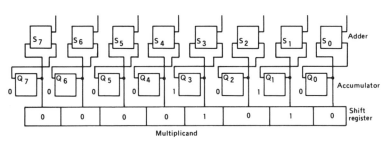

Fig. 7.2

The multiplicand's shift register is next shifted one bit to the left and the multiplier's shift register is shifted one bit to the right. No clock pulses reach the accumulator during these operations so it still contains the first partial product. See Fig. 7.3.

The right-hand bit of the multiplier is then again connected to the ALU ADD control during the next clock pulse. If the right-hand digit of the multiplier is again 1 then this time the shifted multiplicand is added to the contents of the accumulator to give the second

77

partial product. This is carried out for each digit of the multiplier, and the accumulator then contains the final product. If a separate multiply instruction is not provided by the microprocessor then a similar sequence of events can be carried out using the available add and shift instructions in a program subroutine.

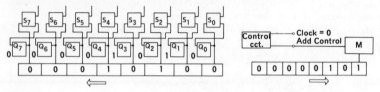

Fig. 7.3

Very large numbers can be handled in a similar way using floating point arithmetic.

Division is carried out by repeated subtraction and shifting in much the same way as multiplication. The subtraction is carried out in 2s complement form and both this and normal pencil and paper subtraction (borrow 2 in binary instead of 10 as in decimal) are shown to try to make it easy to follow. The NEG TEST operation is also made use of in division as the example shows:

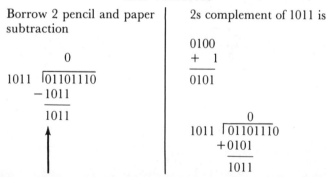

NEG TEST (negative so ignore, shift, and try again) enter 0 in answer.

NEG TEST (not negative so shift and carry on) enter 1 in answer.

78

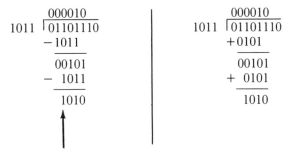

NEG TEST (negative so ignore and shift) enter 0 in answer.

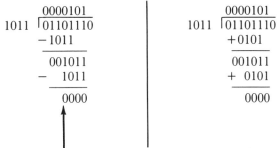

NEG TEST (not negative so enter 1 in answer).

The remainder is now zero so this is the answer, as any further digits must be 0s:

ANS = 00001010

If you look back to the multiplication, 1011 × 1010 was in fact 01101110 so the answer is correct.

What is floating point arithmetic and how does it enable us to handle large magnitude numbers and fractions?

In floating point arithmetic all numbers are scaled so that they are in the form $a \times 2^b$ where for multiplication and division a is less than 1_{10} and the exponent characteristic b is always a whole number (integer). a can be thought of as representing the fractional part of the number because it is less than 1, i.e. a fraction. This is called floating point notation because by varying the exponent characteristic b the decimal point 'floats' (alters position) in the fractional part a.

For example:

binary 10111111000_2 will not fit in an eight-bit register but this can be written as $10111111 \times 2^3{}_{10}$ or $1011.1111 \times 2^7{}_{10}$ or as $.10111111 \times 2^{11}{}_{10}$.

(Note: the exponent is shown in decimal to simplify this example)

Similarly the very small binary number $.000010111111$ can be written as $.10111111 \times 2^{-4}{}_{10}$.

When we store numbers in this way we have to divide the registers up into space for the fractional part, space for the exponent characteristic and two bits (one each) to denote the signs of the fractional part and the exponent part. The exact number of bits used to store each part is determined by the precision required. It is common to use more than one register and memory location to handle more than eight bits for the fractional part and they are then handled in the same way as we saw 16-bit numbers added and subtracted. Each eight-bit word is stored in adjacent memory locations.

Multiplication (division) of numbers in floating point notation is achieved by multiplication (division) of the fractional part and addition (subtraction) of the exponent.

What is meant by multiple and single precision arithmetic?

If we wish to be more accurate then we must use more than one register to store and manipulate our numbers. Single precision usually refers to a single register or memory location being used for each number. Microcomputers can be programmed so that two or more registers and memory locations can be used for each number. This provides greater precision and is called multiple precision arithmetic.

Double precision arithmetic uses two registers.

8
Memory

How does the memory work and what are meant by bit organisaton and word organisation?

Microcomputer memories use semiconductor storage elements (cells) arranged in arrays. Each cell can hold one bit of information (a 1 or a 0). Any particular type of memory chip might have its cells arranged in one of two ways. It can either be organised so that each individual cell can be adressed and read or written into separately (bit organisation), or instead, a fixed number of cells are addressed and read or written into at the same time (word organisation). Typical semiconductor memory chips might have between 256 and 16 384 separate storage elements in one dual in line package.

We have already seen how a flip-flop can be used as a temporary store in registers so let us look next at how a flip-flop can be used in memory of the read/write (RAM) type.

Each memory cell is a simple S-R flip-flop. A logic network such as shown in Fig. 8.1, implemented by a suitable combination of the

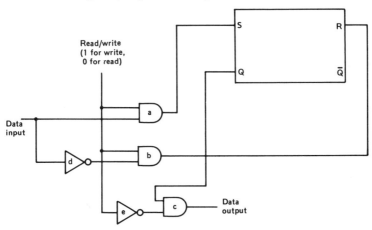

Fig. 8.1. A memory cell

appropriate gates on the memory chip itself, can be used either to route data into the flip-flop for a write, or to read information out from it for a read.

Consider the flip-flop shown in Fig. 8.1. If the read/write line is set to V+ then the two ANDs (a) and (b) each have one input set to V+. Therefore if, at the same time, the data input is set to V+ then the output of (a) is V+ and the output of (b) is zero because the NOT operation (d) inverts the data V+ to a zero.

The flip-flop's set input (S) is therefore V+, and its reset input (R) is zero. So the flip-flop is set and stores a logic 1. During this write, the read/write signal is inverted by the NOT operation (e), therefore AND (c) is disabled and there is no output from it.

Similarly, if the data input is zero at the same time as the read/write line is at V+ then the flip-flop is reset and stores a logic 0.

In order to read from the cell the read/write line has to be made zero. This disables (a) and (b), preventing data from being read in, and enables (c) because the read/write signal is inverted by (e). The output of (c) is therefore equal to the value of Q, i.e. a logic 1 if the flip-flop is set and $Q = V+$, or a logic 0 if the flip-flop is not set and $Q = 0$.

Common microcomputers usually have eight-bit data buses and therefore have to store eight-bit words in each memory location (address). If we use memory chips that are bit organised we require eight of them with their address lines paralleled. The separate data outputs D_7, D_6, D_5, D_4, D_3, D_2, D_1, D_0, are taken one from each chip, as shown in Fig. 8.2.

If each chip contained 256 cells this would give a memory of 256 words × 8 bits each and would require eight address lines (A_0 to A_7). If each chip contained 1024 cells this would give 1 K byte of memory, i.e. 1024 × 8-bit words, and require ten address lines (A_0 to A_9).

Instead we could use word organised chips and these would be connected in a similar manner. The arrangement shown in Fig. 8.3 would give a 256-word × 8-bit memory (¼ K byte) and uses two 256 × 4-bit word memory chips.

Larger memories can be made up from chips by using an input called chip enable (CE). When this input is set at V+ the chip can be written into or read out of, but when chip enable is zero the chip can be neither written into nor read from.

A 1024-word × 4-bit memory can be implemented (as shown in Fig. 8.4) from four 256-word × 4-bit chips even though they only have eight address inputs.

Each memory chip contains a 256-word × 4-bit memory. The A_0 address lines of all the memory chips are connected together.

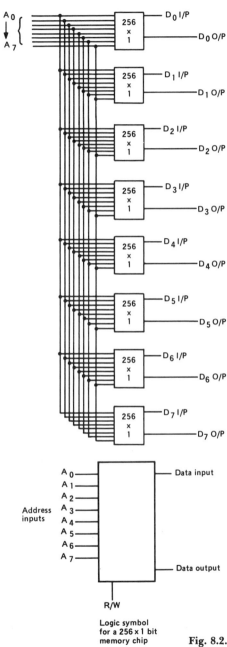

Logic symbol
for a 256 x 1 bit
memory chip

Fig. 8.2. A 256 × 8-bit memory

Fig. 8.3. Logic symbol for a 256 × 4-bit memory chip

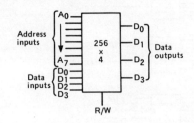

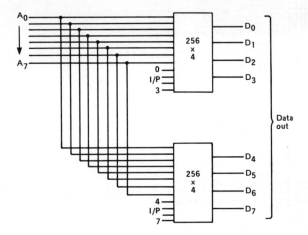

Similarly all the A_1 A_2 A_3 A_4 A_5 A_6 and A_7 address leads are connected to each chip in turn. Signals placed on these address lines will therefore address one word in each of the four memory chips.

The chip enable lines from each chip are not connected together so only the chip whose CE line has a V+ signal on it will actually give an output or be written into. For example, if we want to address word 14 (binary 00001110_2) of chip 3 then the following address signals are required:

A_0	0	A_6	1
A_1	0	A_7	0
A_2	0	CE1	0
A_3	0	CE2	0
A_4	1	CE3	1
A_5	1	CE4	0

84

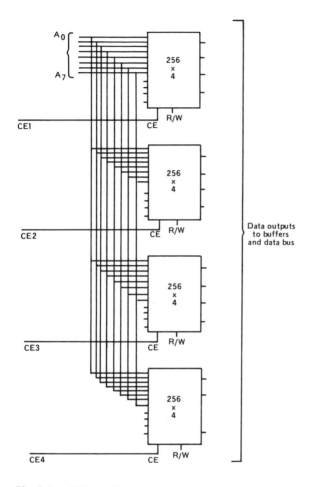

Fig. 8.4. A 1024 × 4-bit memory

How are the chip enable signals derived?

Let's examine the last 1024 × 4-bit memory. 1024 words require ten
address lines ($1024 = 2^{10}$). The first eight, A_0 to A_7, are connected as
shown, and the other two, A_8 and A_9, are used to derive the CE1,
CE2, CE3 and CE4 signals.

Fig. 8.5 shows a circuit that will generate the four chip enable signals required from the two address bus bits A8 and A9.

CE1 will only be $V+$ if $\overline{A9}$ and $\overline{A8}$ are both $V+$, i.e. $A9=A8=0$. CE2, CE3 and CE4 will then have zero outputs. Therefore for addresses

from A9 A8, A7 A6 A5 A4 A3 A2 A1 A0
*   0 0, 0 0 0 0 0 0 0*
up to A9 A8, A7 A6 A5 A4 A3 A2 A1 A0
*   0 0, 1 1 1 1 1 1 1*

only the 256 words stored in chip 1 will be selected. For the next 256 addresses 0 1, 00000000 up to 0 1, 11111111 only the 256 words stored in chip 2 will be selected because an input of $A8 = 1$ and $A9 = 0$ gives $CE1 = 0$, $CE2 = V+$, $CE3 = 0$ and $CE4 = 0$ since (b)'s inputs are $A8 = V+$ and $\overline{A9} = V+$.

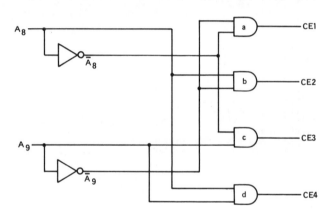

Fig. 8.5

Similarly for addresses from 1 0, 00000000 to 1 0, 11111111 then only the 256 words stored in chip 3 are selected because $\overline{A9} = 1$, $A8 = 0$ gives $CE1 = 0$, $CE2 = 0$, $CE3 = V+$, $CE4 = 0$. For addresses from 1 1, 00000000 up to 1 1, 11111111 only the 256 words stored in chip 4 are selected because $\overline{A9} = 1$, $A8 = 1$ gives $CE1 = 0$, $CE2 = 0$, $CE3 = 0$, $CE4 = V+$.

A 1024-word × 8-bit memory can be achieved in a similar way with two 256 × 4-bit chips paralleled in each of the positions shown in Fig. 8.4. Larger memory systems can be constructed in a similar way using the chip enable input.

Some memory chips have more than one chip enable input and this helps to simplify very large memory systems. For instance, although a microprocessor with a 16-bit address bus can only address 64K bytes of memory, several 64K byte banks can be addressed by paralleling their address lines and then enabling only one of the banks by the use of chip enable inputs selected using an input/output instruction from the microprocessor. This is known as memory bank switching.

One of the latest memory chips is the CMOS-implemented 5101 low-power 1024-bit static RAM which comes in a 22-pin dual-in-line package and requires only a single 5 volt supply.

The chip is word organised as 256 words each four bits long. The storage cell in a chip of this type consists of two of our 'basic inverter units' connected together as an S-R flip-flop (see Chapter 6 'Registers').

A typical memory chip arranged in the same way as the 5101 contains 1024 of these cells arranged as 32 rows by 32 columns.

There are eight address inputs and the first five can be used to address any one of the 32 rows because 11111 is the binary number for 31_{10} and along with the binary address 00000 this gives 32_{10} different addresses:

00000	00001	000010	00011	00100
1	2	3	4	5
....	....	11101	11110	11111
		30	31	32

When one of the addresses is entered at the five address inputs A_4 A_3 A_2 A_1 A_0 it passes through buffers and into a row decoder which sends out a $V+$ along the one appropriate row select line of the 32 possible.

The 32 columns are divided into eight groups of four and any of these eight groups can be addressed by the remaining three address inputs A_5, A_6 and A_7 because 111_2 is decimal 7 and along with zero this gives eight different addresses.

When one of these addresses is entered at the address inputs A_7, A_6 and A_5 it passes through buffers and into a column decoder which only sends a $V+$ signal to the cells in the one appropriate column of the eight possible. Only the one address at the coincidence of the row and column decode outputs is thus enabled. The read/write control signal then determines whether this address is read from or written into. Thus any one of 256 unique four-bit words can be located in the memory chip using a five-bit row address and a three-bit column address.

The actual circuitry for selecting, and then reading from, or writing into, each cell varies from one memory chip type to another.

What happens to all the data inputs and outputs from each cell?

The D_0 inputs to the first cells in each column of each row are connected together and go to the D_0 chip input. The other cells are connected to the appropriate chip inputs. Data at the chip inputs is only written into those cells whose columns and rows are simultaneously enabled by the address inputs.

All the D_0 outputs from each column and each row are 'OR'ed' together and then connected to the D_0 chip output. The other data outputs from the other cells are connected in the same way to their respective chip outputs. Data is only read from those cells whose columns and rows are simultaneously enabled.

How are the memory chips themselves connected to the data bus?

Connection of memory chips to the data bus can be achieved with multi-input OR gates. However, some chips have on-chip Tri-State Output (TSO) buffers. (Tri-State is a trademark of National Semiconductors Ltd.) These eliminate the need for OR gates and enable them to be connected directly in parallel with all the other memory chips. Tri-state output means that they can either have an output of $V+$ for a logic 1, of zero for a logic 0, or go high impedance (high Z) when the chip is not being read from, which effectively is like unplugging the output from the data bus.

How are these three states achieved?

They are implemented in CMOS by a tri-state buffer whose logic is such that a complementary pair of P and N channel MOSFETs can either be turned on one at a time, or both off at the same time. See Fig. 8.6.

One tri-state buffer is required on each data output line. Output enable is set to $V+$ to enable the output, and to zero to disable the output, and set it to high impedance.

If there is a zero on the data line we want the buffer output to be zero when output enable $(OE) = V+$ and it will be if the N channel MOSFET is on, i.e. its gate is at $V+$, and the P channel MOSFET is off, i.e. its gate is also at $V+$.

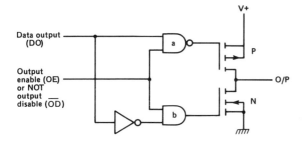

Logic symbol for above tri-state buffer

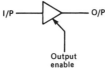

Fig. 8.6. A tri-state buffer

If (a)'s inputs are 0 and V+ its output is V+. The inputs to (b) are both V+ therefore its output is V+. The P channel MOSFET is therefore OFF and the N channel MOSFET is ON so the buffer output is zero.

If now the data output is V+ and OE is V+ then the P channel MOSFET is ON and the N channel MOSFET is OFF. The buffer output is therefore V+.

If at any time output enable is zero then no matter what the data input is the output of (a) will be V+ and the output of (b) will be zero so both the MOSFETs will be off.

The resistance of a MOSFET when off is about one million million ohms (10^{12}) so the output is effectively unplugged from the data bus and is said to be high impedance.

How do the address decoders work?

Binary addresses are used because this reduces the number of external address lines required. For instance, a ten-line address input to a memory chip can uniquely define 1024 different addresses within that chip.

When the binary address reaches the memory chip via the address bus it has to be decoded to provide a signal to a particular row and column. This can be achieved quite simply by using logic gates in a similar fashion to the way that the chip enable signals were derived.

When the address reaches the memory chip it is often latched into a register of flip-flops which allows the address to be present on the address bus for only a short time but available to the memory decoder for longer. This register also automatically produces the complement of the address at its $\overline{Q}$ outputs. If a particular memory chip does not contain flip-flops it must have NOT gates to produce the complement of the address because this is used by the decoder.

Consider the simple case where we want to address a four-row by four-column, 16-bit, memory array. We therefore require two row address inputs to give four row addresses 00, 01, 10 and 11 and two column address inputs to give four column addresses. This will produce 16 unique one-bit locations in memory. The row and column select signals can be derived from the binary addresses by a logic implementation such as that shown in Fig. 8.7.

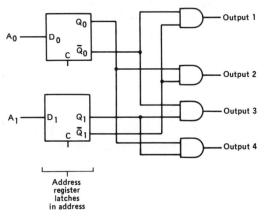

Fig. 8.7

The clock connections to the address register are not shown. It is possible to connect the clock pulses via control circuits so that they are only applied to the register when it is required to change the stored address.

This circuit works in the same way as the chip enable circuit previously described. Other decode circuits implemented with different gates may be encountered. For instance, the 5101 memory chip uses AND gates for its row decoder but NOR gates to decode its three column addresses to select one of eight columns.

Sometimes you will see a chip select signal referred to. This is used to enable the address decoders of a particular chip when it is selected.

What are meant by static, dynamic, and volatile memories?

The type of memory described so far will store information without the need for any refreshing and is therefore said to be static. However, information is lost if the power is switched off so it is said to be volatile.

A common type of static RAM is the 2102 sixteen-pin dual-in-line 1024×1-bit NMOS RAM. This uses cross-coupled N MOSFETs to store information.

Each memory cell consists of four N channel MOSFETs (see Fig. 8.8).

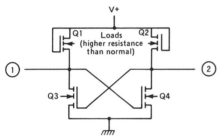

Fig. 8.8. The 2102 'basic' memory cell. This is a pair of NMOS inverters arranged as a flip-flop

Data is stored as a positive charge on the gate of either Q_3 or Q_4 where it turns the appropriate MOSFET on.

Assume Q_3 is ON, i.e. positive charge is stored on its gate. Current can now flow through Q_1 to ground. Point (1) is therefore near zero volts. (The actual value depends on the ratio of the resistances of Q_1 and Q_2 when they are on.) Q_4's gate is therefore at, or very near, zero volts so Q_4 is OFF. Q_2 maintains the charge on the gate of Q_3 by replacing any charge that might leak away. The storage cell will therefore remain in this logic state until it is changed by a write and this also applies if Q_4 is on and Q_3 is off.

Another common type of RAM cell is dynamic RAM in which data is stored as a charge on a capacitor. A three transistor NMOS dynamic memory cell is shown in Fig. 8.9.

MOSFET Q_4 is common to all memory cells in a column of the array and is used to pre-charge capacitor C_D.

To read from the cell, C_D is first pre-charged to a voltage very close to $V+$. This is achieved by MOSFET Q_4 whose gate is connected to NOT CHIP ENABLE. The read line which is common to a row of the array is set to $V+$ and this turns on Q_3. If the voltage stored on C_G is a logic 1 (i.e. very nearly $V+$), Q_2 is ON and so C_D is discharged via Q_3 and Q_2 to ground. If, however, the voltage stored on C_G is a logic 0 (i.e. 0 volts), Q_2 is OFF and so C_D remains charged at $V+$. Hence the complement of the data stored appears on the read data line.

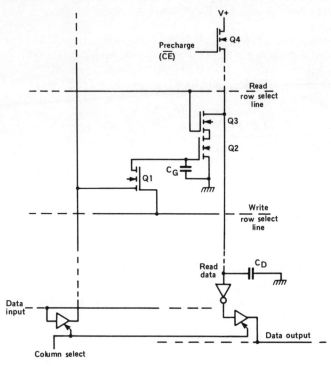

Fig. 8.9. An NMOS dynamic memory cell

Notice that the state of C_G remains unaltered during a read. The data may be read from C_D, complemented, and latched into an output register, or sent out on the data bus via a suitable buffer.

To write into the cell the write row select line is set to $V+$ instead of the read row select line. (There is often only one combined read/write input.)

The write row select line is common to a row of the cell array and turns on Q_1 in each cell in the row, which transfers the voltage present on the write data line of the selected column to the one selected cell's capacitor C_G.

The read row select and write row select signals for each row can be obtained by 'ANDing' the read and write signals with the appropriate row select signals from the row decoder.

92

Although readout is not destructive the charge on capacitor C_G deteriorates because of leakage. It therefore has to be refreshed by special refresh circuitry that reads the contents of the cell and writes it back in to the same cell at frequent intervals. This circuitry is incorporated on the Z80 MPU chip but more usually has to be provided separately.

How is read only memory constructed?

Read only memory (ROM) can be thought of as an array of selectively open or closed unidirectional contacts (which only pass current one way) as shown in Fig. 8.10.

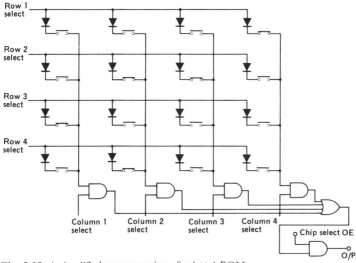

Fig. 8.10. A simplified representation of a 4 × 4 ROM

Notice that it is very similar to RAM but of course there is no write circuitry. The row and column select lines are obtained from the address lines in the same way as for RAMs and individual 'cells' are addressed and read from in much the same way as in RAM.

Different types of ROM exist and their major differences are in the way the open or closed contacts are formed. In mask programmed ROMs the contacts are selectively made or excluded during the final stages of production.

In programmable read only memories (PROM) the contact is constructed from fusible material that can later be opened allowing the information stored to be programmed by the user after the device has been manufactured.

Erasable programmable ROMs (EPROM) allow the programmed contacts to be restored to their original states and then reprogrammed.

There are two basic technologies in existence, bipolar and MOS. Their primary difference is access time. (Time taken for the data at a specific address to become available.) Bipolar access times are about ten times faster than MOS. Bipolar transistor circuits take up more room on the chip than equivalent MOS circuits and are available in 1 K, 2 K and 4 K bit sizes. MOS ROMs are available in sizes up to 16 K bits.

EPROMs are only manufactured in MOS technology.

ROMs

Bipolar (60 ns)   MOS (500 ns)

MASK ROMs PROMs   MASK   PROMs EPROMs
                         ROMs

PROMs

SILICON   NICHROME   SHORTED
FUSE   FUSE   JUNCTION

The first electrically programmable read only memories (PROMs) used nichrome fuses and heavy currents were used to blow these open during their programming. Each cell consisted of a bipolar transistor switch and a fuse, as shown in Fig. 8.11.

If the row is selected during a read then row select = V+, the transistor switch is ON and if the fuse is intact then the column is connected to V+ and gives an output of V+ when 'AND'ed' with column select at the foot of the selected column. If the fuse is blown the output of the selected column is zero.

Nichrome fuse PROMs suffered from 'growback', i.e. after a period of time some of the fuses reconnected. This problem has been overcome by using polycrystalline silicon as the fuse material instead of nichrome.

ROMs and PROMs are also produced using MOSFETs in place of bipolar transistors. However erasable PROMs are *only* produced with MOS transistors of a special type known as Floating Gate Avalanche-injection Metal Oxide Semiconductor transistors (FAMOS). Think of these as P channel MOSFETs with no external connection to their gates.

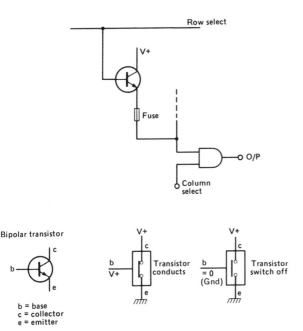

Fig. 8.11. A bipolar PROM

A source/drain voltage in excess of -30 volts results in high energy electrons being injected, by a process known as avalanche-injection, into the gate from either the source or the drain. Once on the gate the negative charge of the electrons produces an electric field in the channel which tends to switch the P channel MOSFET on. (That is, to increase its conductance between source and drain.)

When the programming voltage is removed, no discharge path is available to the electrons on the gate as it is surrounded by insulating silicon dioxide. The electrons therefore stay on the gate. Tests show that the silicon dioxide is such a good insulator that over 70 per cent of the charge would remain on the gate even after ten years. There are no electrical connections to the gate so the electrons cannot be removed by electrical means.

However, if the FAMOS device is illuminated by ultraviolet light the electrons absorb sufficient energy to jump back to the silicon substrate. The gate is thus discharged and the cell returns to its unprogrammed condition. EPROMs can thus be programmed and used as ROM but later, if required, they can be reprogrammed after exposure to ultraviolet light. EPROMs are very useful for producing one-off special prototype ROMs.

Another type of EPROM cell is the stacked-gate single transistor cell used in the 2708 EPROM chip. This has a bottom floating gate and a top select gate connected to the row select line.

The cell is programmed by avalanche-injection of electrons to the floating gate. As this is an N channel MOSFET the electric field produced by the negative charge on the floating gate tends to reduce the conductivity of the MOSFET when it is selected. It would therefore require a lager select gate positive voltage to turn it on than an unprogrammed cell. This fact is used for data storage.

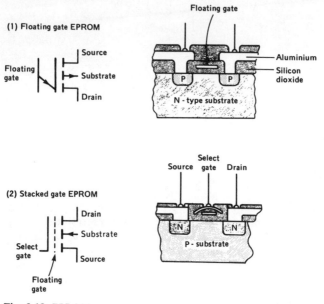

Fig. 8.12. EPROM

Sufficient charge is injected on to the floating gate to ensure that only the unprogrammed cells are selected by the select voltage. The cell can be erased by exposure to ultra-violet light of the correct frequency.

All ROM, PROM, and EPROM are non-volatile. That is, information is *not* lost when the power is switched off.

What are backing store memories such as tape cassettes and floppy disks used for?

These are useful because they are non-volatile and large quantities of data and programs can be stored permanently on them ready for future use. If we wish to store data on a cassette (i.e. create a file) then access time can be slow, especially if the data required is near the end of the tape, because the whole of the tape has to be scanned through before the required data is found.

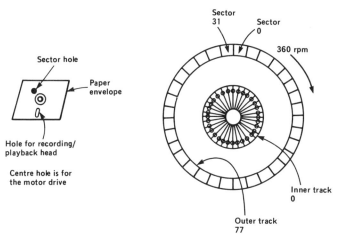

Fig. 8.13. The IBM 3740 disc system (capable of holding up to 243 000 bytes). This system uses one sector hole for each sector (a hard sectored disc) and hardware locates the correct sector. Some systems have only one sector hole and software then locates the other sectors (a soft sectored disc)

This is overcome in the floppy disk which stores data in magnetic form on a disk kept, and used, in a thin paper envelope. The data is recorded in serial concentric tracks. (Not in a spiral like a record.) Each track is divided into segments. The read/record head can be positioned directly to any sector of any track under software control. This greatly reduces access time compared with a cassette tape. It is, however, slower than semiconductor RAM and ROM.

What is bubble memory?

Another type of magnetic memory falling between RAM and floppy disk is the bubble memory. Small bubbles, or regions of magnetism, are formed in a sheet of magnetic material. These can be read in serial form. Bubble memories are non-volatile and their greatest advantage is that large quantities of information can be stored cheaply in a small area – more than one million bits in one square centimetre. Bubble memories give huge amounts of storage but at the expense of very high speed.

What is meant by page addressing?

All memory has to be addressed by the address bus. If this is a 16-bit address bus then each address can be represented by 16 binary digits or four hexadecimal digits (see Chapter 3). For instance:

1101   0010   1011   1110
D   2   B   E

The first half of the address is referred to as the page number and the second half as the displacement in the page. Eight binary digits therefore represent $2^8 = 256$ pages and each has 256 locations represented by the least significant eight binary digits of the address.

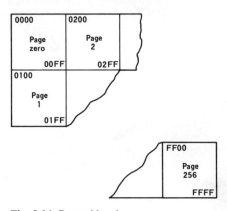

Fig. 8.14. Page addressing

Page zero is thus addresses with the first two hex digits zero, 00 00 to 00 FF (0–255$_{10}$). Page 1 is addresses from 01 00 to 01 FF (256$_{10}$–511$_{10}$), page 2 addresses from 02 00 to 02 FF (512$_{10}$–767$_{10}$) and so on up to page 256 which is addresses from FF 00 to FF FF (65 281$_{10}$–65 535$_{10}$).

What is a memory map?

This is a diagram showing where, in the 65 536 possible addresses, particular types of the microcomputer's memory are located. The memory map often also conveys other information about the use of particular memory addresses. It is important to stick to the manufacturer's recommendations as there must be memory of the

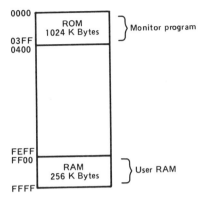

Fig. 8.15. A memory map

ROM type at the address that the MPU returns to after being reset (e.g. 00 00) in order to give the microcomputer its initial intelligence.

What is meant by memory mapping?

This is a technique of implementing input and output from the microcomputer by addressing input and output ports as if they were memory locations. So addressing external devices is the same as reading or writing to memory. Some systems provide separate input and output instructions instead of using memory mapping I/O techniques.

What is meant by addressing modes?

The memory is used to store op-codes, addresses, data for manipulation, and results. In order for the MPU to be able to execute an instruction it needs to be told: 1. the op-code, 2. the location of the first operand (or the operand itself), 3. the location of the second operand (or the operand itself), 4. the location in which to place the result.

All four items could be contained in every instruction but it is not usual to do this because of the length of the instruction word required. Often the destination (4) is implied by the op-code, as for example in the instruction LDA where 'into the accumulator' is implied.

Sometimes items 2 and 3 are implied, or not required, as in our INC where 'the accumulator and place the result back in the accumulator' is implied and no other operand is required.

The different ways of specifying the location of the operand are known as addressing modes.

'Direct' addressing modes give the absolute address of the oper- and and 'indirect' addressing modes enable the absolute address to be found by some indirect means. A typical microprocessor uses an eight-bit op-code and 16-bit addresses. Typical instructions range from one byte (eight bits) to three bytes. Different microprocessors allow different addressing modes and unfortunately different manu- facturers sometimes give different names to the same addressing modes. In general, the smaller the instruction set the greater the number of addressing modes that can be provided. It is the combination of different addressing modes and the actual instruc- tions that determine the computing power of any particular micro- processor.

What are the common addressing modes I am likely to encoun- ter?

Direct addressing

In direct addressing the address of the operand is given in the instruction after the op-code. Sometimes only one byte of address need be used and the operand must therefore be on page zero. The instruction is then a two byte instruction, the first byte is the op-code and the second byte the least significant eight bits of the address.

When a full 16-bit address is given then the addressing mode is sometimes called extended addressing. For instance, in the previous three-byte example:

Instruction meaning	'Typical' instruction op-code – address
LOAD the accumulator with the contents of memory location ** **	AD ** **

Accumulator addressing

This is a one-byte instruction that always operates on the accumula- tor. No further address is therefore required, only the op-code. E.g.

Instruction meaning	'Typical' instruction op-code
COMPLEMENT the accumulator	17

Immediate addressing

The operand itself is the second byte of the instruction. This addressing mode is useful when it is necessary to perform arithmetic or logic with constant data. E.g.

Instruction meaning	'Typical' instruction op-code − data
ADD nn to the accumulator (where nn is an eight-bit binary data word).	6E nn

Indirect addressing

The instruction contains either a memory address, or an internal register address, that contains the address of the operand. (Each memory location can only contain an eight-bit word so unless register indirect addressing is used the operand must be on page zero.) E.g.

Instruction meaning	'Typical' instruction op-code − address
LOAD the accumulator with the data in the memory location indicated by the contents of the address ** **	3A ** **

Sometimes a full 16-bit address is contained in two adjacent memory locations and the instruction might then be: LOAD the accumulator with the data in the memory location indicated by ** ** and ** ** + 1.

Indexed addressing

The address contained in the second byte of the instruction is combined with the contents of a register called the index register to produce the address of the operand. This addressing mode is useful when the same sequence of calculaions has to be performed on different sets of data stored in a series of memory locations. E.g.

Instruction meaning	'Typical' instruction op-code
LOAD the word in the memory location given by the contents of the index register + the eight bit word ** into the accumulator	AE **

Implied addressing

A one-byte instruction where the operation code is fixed and the instruction itself implies the address and always performs exactly the same operation. E.g.

Instruction meaning	'Typical' op-code
LOAD the stack pointer (a register in the MPU) with the contents of register X.	AF

Relative addressing

The address contained in the second byte of the instruction is combined with the program counter's contents to produce the operand's address. This can be used for branch instructions. Sometimes the second byte (the displacement) has to be in 2s complement form and this allows jumps backwards or forwards (i.e. program counter $\pm$ displacement). The new address formed can be the program counter $+ 127_{10}$ to the program counter $- 128_{10}$. E.g.

Instruction meaning	'Typical' instruction op-code – displacement
Fetch the next instruction from the memory location given by the contents of the program counter register and the eight-bit word dd.	10 dd

9
Control

What are control signals?

The arithmetic and logic unit (ALU) performs operations selected
by a set of control signals such as ADD, CLEAR, INC, etc. These
control signals are generated by the control unit within the microprocessor. The control unit receives its instructions, in the form of
binary codes, from the program and it then generates the appropriate control signals in the correct sequence and at the proper times.
The control unit controls the supply of data to and from the input
and output devices and the various other parts of the microcomputer
as well as directing the reading and writing functions of the memory.
It contains the master clock which synchronises the operation of all
the parts of the microcomputer.

The clock lines, the address bus, data bus, chip enable, power
lines, read/write lines and other control lines make up the total bus
structure. All of the bus lines do not *need* to go to every part of the
computer, but for practical reasons it is convenient to run all the bus
lines to all parts of the computer and thus provide a very versatile
arrangement that gives easy access to all the bus lines. There may be
50 to 100 individual lines in a typical microcomputer bus structure,
and these are often arranged as a set of parallel printed circuit strips
on a circuit board called the motherboard or backplane. The other
boards containing the MPU, memory, etc. can be plugged into the
motherboard by means of edge connectors.

What parts of the MPU are used for control and the movement of data?

Inside a 'typical' MPU is a register acting as a memory address
register, or memory address pointer. It is used during an instruction
execution to store the address of the memory location to be
addressed by the address bus. The addresses are 16 bits long so this
register must be a 16-bit register (or two eight-bit registers could be

used.). The memory address pointer register can also be used to build up or manipulate an address during the execution of an instruction.

Another register, sometimes called a buffer register, is used to store the word that is to be written into memory or that has just been read from a memory location.

When a program instruction is encountered the op-code is stored in a register in the MPU called the instruction register (IR). The op-code stored in the instruction register instructs the microprocessor to perform a specific operation. An instruction decoder converts the op-code stored in the instruction register into the appropriate control signals and the control unit supplies the correct sequence of signals to the appropriate parts of the microcomputer in order to execute the instruction.

For instance, if the op-code for ADD is 6D (i.e. $0110\ 1101_2$) and for CLEAR is 18 (i.e. $0001\ 1000_2$), then the logic implementation shown in Fig. 9.1 would produce ADD and CLEAR signals when, and only when, the instruction register contained the correct op-codes $Q_7Q_6Q_5Q_4Q_3Q_2Q_1Q_0$. *When the op-code is $0110\ 1101_2$ every input to (a) is $V+$ and therefore its output is $V+$. Any other op-code gives at least one input to (a) of zero so its output is zero. Similarly for (b) which only gives an output for an op-code of $0001\ 1000_2$.*

Any transfer of data required for the execution of an instruction also requires correctly sequenced control signals to be supplied by the control section. For instance, the instruction ADD also requires data to be transferred from memory to the arithmetic and logic unit. How the control section generates the particular sequence of control signals required for different instructions is explained later.

During the execution of a program the binary word stored in each memory location can represent either data to be manipulated, an instruction, or the address of another location. It is the order in which the words are written and read that indicates which they represent and the microprocessor has to keep track of this order.

For example, 6D CB 00 might represent ADD the contents of memory location 00 CB to the accumulator. The first two hexadecimal digits 6D represent an instruction op-code and the next four CB 00 represent an address in memory. When this address is read its contents represent data to be manipulated.

The MPU will contain an internal flag, which is a one-bit register, that can be used to indicate if the MPU is to fetch part of an instruction from memory or to execute an instruction. This fetch flag is sometimes called a fetch/execute register. If the flag is set, i.e. a 1 is stored, then the microcomputer treats the word being read from memory as part of an instruction. If the flag is not set, i.e. a zero is

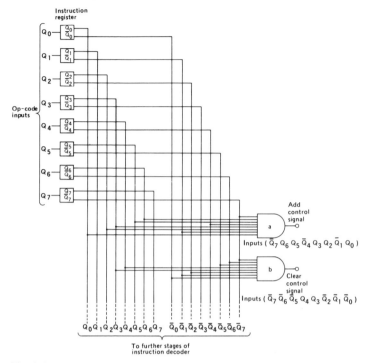

Fig. 9.1. An instruction decoder

stored, then the word is treated as data to be manipulated. This flag is not available to the user and we need not concern ourselves with it any further.

There is also a register called a program counter (PC) which holds the address of the next instruction to be fetched. The addresses are 16-bit words so two eight-bit registers within the MPU are often used as the program counter. One is used for the LOW or least significant eight address bits (PCL) and one for the HIGH or most significant eight address bits (PCH). When an instruction is executed the program goes through a series of steps during the processing of data. One of these steps increases the number stored in the program counter until it indicates the location of the next instruction to be fetched.

When the program is run a typical sequence of events might be as follows. First the program counter is set to the address of the start of the first instruction. The contents of this address are next fetched and treated as an instruction op-code. That is, they are placed in the instruction register (IR) where they will cause the appropriate

105

control signal to be generated when connected to the instruction decoder. The program counter is incremented and, if the op-code signifies a direct addressing mode, then the contents of this memory location are fetched and placed in the least significant eight digits of the memory pointer register. The program counter is incremented again and, if the op-code indicates a three-byte instruction, the contents of the address now given by the program counter are fetched and placed in the memory address pointer's most significant eight digits. The instruction fetch is now complete.

The contents of the address in the memory address pointer register are read into the memory buffer register, and the operation designated by the op-code, still stored in the instruction register, is carried out. The program counter is incremented, and the word contained in the memory location now indicated by the program counter is fetched and treated as the next instruction op-code. The process is repeated until the stop instruction is encountered.

The exact sequence of events will vary with different instructions and addressing modes. The program counter can also be incremented or decremented by more than one instruction address and the program made to jump out of sequence. The program sequence can thus be made to depend on certain conditions that can be tested for, such as equality, zero, negative, greater than, etc.

The MPU usually also contains a register known as the stack pointer (SP). This contains the address of, that is it points to, the bottom of the stack. The stack is an area of memory set aside for temporary storage of the registers inside the MPU. This is required if we wish to jump out of sequence and later return, for example to execute a subroutine or for an interrupt. The current contents of the program counter and, in the case of an interrupt, other registers have to be stored so that the microprocessor can return, and continue, from where it left off. (If the stack pointer is an eight-bit register note that the stack is limited to 256 locations in page 1.) Data from the MPU is 'pushed' into the top of the stack area eight bits at a time and the SP decreased by one so that it always indicates the bottom of the stack.

When data is retrieved from the stack ('popped') the stack pointer is incremented by one for each byte popped. This is known as a 'last-in-first-out' (LIFO) stack. (Some people say pull instead of pop.)

There may also be index registers in the MPU that allow indexed addressing in programs. The index register is used to calculate the effective memory address of the operand during the execution of an instruction by combining the contents of the index register and another number contained in the instruction address itself.

There may also be an interrupt vector register that can be loaded with data which, when combined with data from an interrupting device, such as an input port, represents a memory address that points to the location of a software interrupt routine for that device. For instance, the input port can tell the MPU it is ready to transfer data, interrupt the main program and cause the MPU to go to another program subroutine to handle the transfer of the data. When data transfer is complete the MPU can return to the main program.

The parts of the MPU referred to so far are shown in Fig. 9.2 which represents a 'typical' microprocessor's internal architecture.

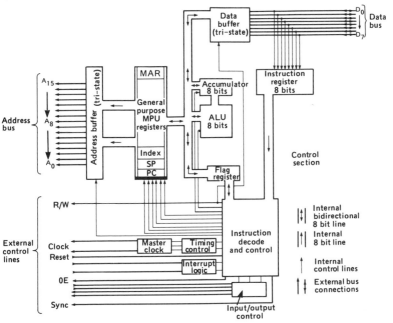

Fig. 9.2. Microprocessor architecture

As we have already noted the microcomputer cannot distinguish between data to be manipulated and instructions to be executed. If the programmer accidentally places data in memory where the microprocessor expects an instruction, or vice versa, an error will occur and if the microprocessor does not find a valid instruction it will stop. If by chance the instruction is valid, but is the wrong instruction, it will be executed but the answer will not be what the programmer expected. After writing a program the programmer has

107

to go through it step by step and correct any such mistakes. This is known as debugging the program.

What is meant by interrupt?

An interrupt signals the MPU that an external event has occurred and requires attention. Suppose that data is being transferred from an external serial source to the microcomputer. Each eight bits have to be read into the input port in serial form one at a time before the MPU can handle them in parallel. There will therefore be a time lag between each new data byte (eight bits) becoming available. During this gap the MPU is simply continually querying the input port to see whether the next byte is available. This is wasteful as the MPU has to be idle waiting for each byte of data.

Interrupts allow the MPU to use the idle time to execute another part of the program. When each data byte is available the interrupt action informs the MPU and an interrupt sequence is entered which allows some processing of the data before the MPU returns to the interrupted part of the program.

Several input/output ports can be handled at the same time by the use of vectored interrupts which also indicate which device requires attention.

Interrupts are also used to allow real-time working. This is when data is processed quickly enough for the information produced to be used in controlling the activity currently putting the data into the microcomputer.

Other interrupts are used to signal abnormal or catastrophic conditions such as an imminent power failure or failure of part of the system. These types of interrupts are non-maskable which means that they are unconditionally implemented immediately at the end of the current instruction.

What is the clock?

The clock provides a series of pulses at regular intervals. One clock cycle is often referred to as a T state.

The clock can be constructed quite simply by using inverters. Consider the theoretical oscillator shown in Fig. 9.3.

If point (a) is set at $V+$ (logic 1) then point (b) goes to zero (logic 0), point (c) goes to $V+$ and point (d) goes to zero. This sets point (a) to zero so point (b) goes to $V+$, (c) goes to zero, and (d) to $V+$, and so on with a $V+$ (logic 1) chasing itself round the ring. The

Output

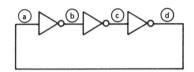

V+ — —

0 — —

⟵ T state ⟶
1 clock
cycle

Theoretical circuit

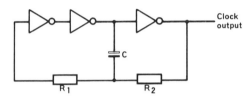

A practical circuit

Clock
output

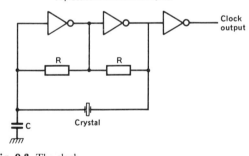

A practical circuit with a crystal

Clock
output

R   R

C   Crystal

Fig. 9.3. The clock

frequency of oscillation depends on the propagation delay of the inverters. Any odd number of inverters will oscillate in this way and all we have to do to make a useful oscillator, or clock, is slow the oscillation down to the desired frequency. This can be done with a capacitor which does not allow the input to which it is connected to change state instantly. The capacitor has first to charge or discharge. So by choosing suitable values for R and C in the circuit the frequency of oscillation can be determined.

If $R1 = R2$, $F = \dfrac{0.599}{RC}$ Hz

R in ohms
C in farads

When high stability is required, such as when a microprocessor is being operated close to its maximum frequency, a crystal can be used in the circuit to ensure that the precise frequency is maintained by the clock.

How does the clock control the microprocessor?

Each MPU instruction can be broken down into a series of basic operations such as memory read or write. Each of these basic operations, called machine cycles, takes several clock cycles and consists of two principal parts, a fetch phase and an execute phase. Just as the complete instruction can be broken down into machine cycles so the machine cycles can be broken down into micro-operations such as enable program counter register output, send ADD signal to ALU, etc.

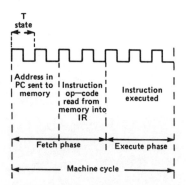

Fig. 9.4. Timing for an instruction requiring only one machine cycle

Some instructions only require one machine cycle and are executed during the first machine cycle execute phase, e.g. CLEAR carry flag shown in Fig. 9.4.

An instruction whose op-code and related address occupy more than one location in memory requires more than one machine cycle

110

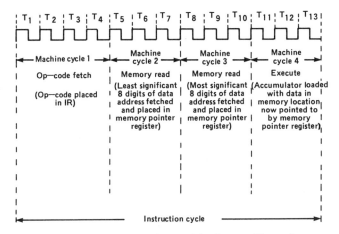

Fig. 9.5. Timing for an instruction requiring four machine cycles

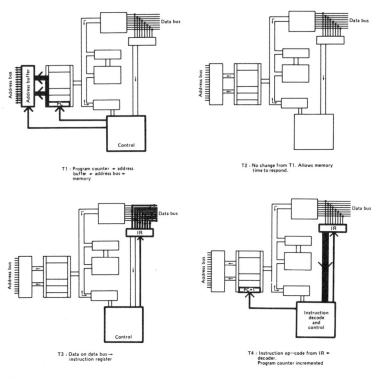

T1 : Program counter → address
buffer → address bus →
memory

T2 : No change from T1. Allows memory
time to respond.

T3 : Data on data bus →
instruction register

T4 : Instruction op—code from IR →
decoder.
Program counter incremented

Fig. 9.6a. Machine cycle 1

111

before fetching is complete. The MPU is either idle during these machine cycle fetch phases, or the fetch phases are omitted, until the complete instruction has been fetched. Subsequent machine cycles then execute the instruction. All data transfer takes place during the fetch phases of machine cycles. Fig. 9.5 represents an instruction such as LOAD 102 being fetched and executed. Fig. 9.6a, b, c and d show the breakdown of each machine cycle.

Each machine cycle requires a carefully-timed sequence of control pulses to activate the correct data paths at the correct times and produce the correct micro-operations. These control pulses could be generated in the instruction decoder control section, from the op-code, by hardware logic and sequence generators made up from flip-flops and gates. However this requires very extensive circuitry. Less circuitry is required if a read only memory (ROM) is used to store the 1s that produce the control pulses. Several 'microinstruction words' could be stored in the correct order for each instruction and a counter could be used to read each control word in sequence onto the control lines.

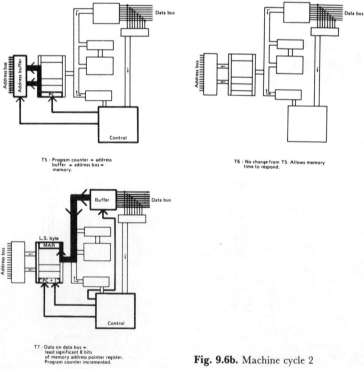

T5 : Program counter → address
buffer → address bus →
memory.

T6 : No change from T5. Allows memory
time to respond.

T7 : Data on data bus →
least significant 8 bits
of memory address pointer register.
Program counter incremented.

Fig. 9.6b. Machine cycle 2

Different instructions could be catered for by using a separate ROM for each instruction and using the instruction decoder outputs to enable only the required ROM.

Rather a large amount of ROM is required for a useful instruction set. In 1952 Wilkes and Stringer suggested the use of a microprogram, contained in the ROM, to provide the sequencing as well as the control pulses. This is what a microprocessor control section uses. The instruction decoder and control section form a dedicated task 'microprocessor within a microprocessor'. The microprogrammed decoder contains a control ROM which has been programmed during manufacture with microinstructions for its particular instruction set. Each user level machine language op-code is decoded and gives the starting address in the microprogram for that instruction. Part of the machine language op-code is also used to determine where the microprogram will jump to whatever subroutines are required by that particular instruction.

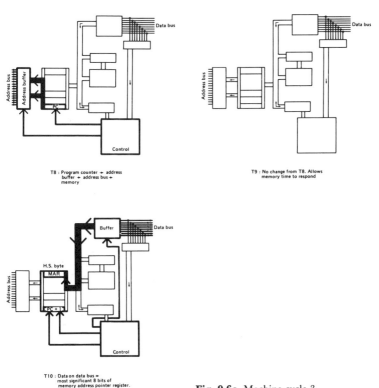

T8 : Program counter → address
buffer → address bus →
memory

T9 : No change from T8. Allows
memory time to respond

T10 : Data on data bus →
most significant 8 bits of
memory address pointer register.
Program counter incremented.

Fig. 9.6c. Machine cycle 3

113

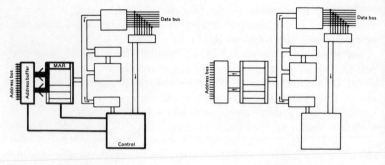

T11 : Memory address pointer
register → address buffer
→ memory

T12 : No change from T11. Allows
memory time to respond

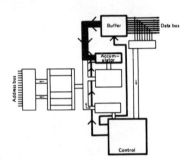

T13 : Data on data bus → Buffer →
accumulator.

Fig. 9.6d. Machine cycle 4

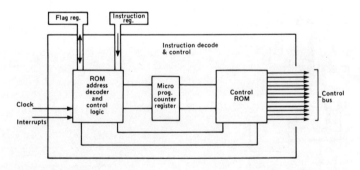

Fig. 9.7

Branching can also depend on the conditions of the flags in the flag register. The use of subroutines enables the amount of ROM required to be drastically reduced and it is all contained on the microprocessor chip in the control section. As the microprogram is executed the microinstructions are read out in the correct order and perform the required micro-operations. Fig. 9.7 shows such a system.

What is meant by a two-phase clock?

Some microprocessors require an external clock and this can be either single-phase or two-phase. Two-phase simply means that the clock has two outputs that are out of phase with each other; that is, they are not always at the same voltage levels at the same time as each other. Fig. 9.8 shows two outputs that are exactly out of phase with each other. When one is at $V+$ the other is always at zero.

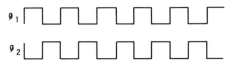

Fig. 9.8. Two-phase clock outputs

Often the master clock signal is used to generate slower clock signals used in other, slower, parts of the microcomputer such as the memory. Faster parts of the microcomputer are thus able to carry out several operations for each cycle of the slower parts.

What other control circuits might I come across?

You will probably come across the multiplexer. This is a digitally-controlled switch that is able to connect one, or none, of its inputs to its output depending on the control signals it receives. Multiplexers are used to connect parts of the microcomputer that do not have tri-state outputs. This prevents contention on the bus lines.

A uni-directional multiplexer can be constructed from AND and OR gates or from tri-state output buffers described in Chapter 8. Fig. 9.9 shows such a tri-state buffer.

Bi-directional multiplexers can be constructed that allow the flow of data in both directions, but only in one direction at a time, and Fig. 9.10 shows such a multiplexer.

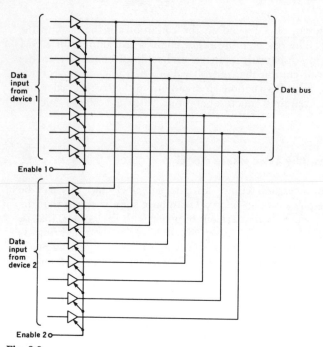

Fig. 9.9

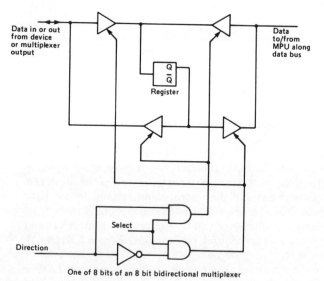

One of 8 bits of an 8 bit bidirectional multiplexer

Fig. 9.10. A bidirectional multiplexer

116

When the direction control signal is zero (e) is disabled so its output is zero and tri-state buffers (c) and (b) are disabled, but (f) is enabled due to inverter (g). If the multiplexer is selected then the output of (f) will be V+ so tri-state buffers (d) and (a) will be enabled. Data can thus be read from the left into the multiplexer register and out again to the MPU.

Similarly if the direction control is at V+ data can be transferred from the MPU through buffer (b) into the multiplexer register and out through buffer (c).

When the select signal is zero all tri-state buffers go high impedance and data transfer cannot take place in either direction.

10
Input/output

How do microcomputers read input and display output?

The simplest form of output display consists of eight light-emitting diodes (LEDs) connected to the data bus.

Seven-segment LED displays are slightly more complicated. These produce a decimal figure by selective illumination of their segments. They have to be driven by suitable drivers that convert the binary output of the data bus to the correct combination of the seven output drive lines to produce the equivalent decimal display.

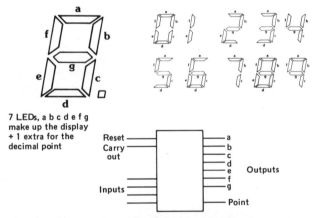

7 LEDs, a b c d e f g make up the display + 1 extra for the decimal point

Reset ——
Carry out ——
Inputs ——

—— a
—— b
—— c
—— d
—— e Outputs
—— f
—— g
—— Point

Fig. 10.1. A seven segment LED display

On the input side of the microcomputer, if anything other than one simple switch per binary digit is used to input data, some sort of code is required to convey the information in binary form. Numbers could be represented by their binary equivalents but letters and punctuation require a special code. The most common code used in microcomputers is the American Standard Code for Information Interchange (ASCII). ASCII can be used to represent alphanumeric, special, and control characters.

Symbol	7 BIT ASCII	Symbol	7 BIT ASCII
A	100 0001	a	110 0001
B	100 0010	b	110 0010
C	100 0011	c	110 0011
D	100 0100	d	110 0100
E	100 0101	e	110 0101
F	100 0110	f	110 0110
G	100 0111	g	110 0111
H	100 1000	h	110 1000
I	100 1001	i	110 1001
J	100 1010	j	110 1010
K	100 1011	k	110 1011
L	100 1100	l	110 1100
M	100 1101	m	110 1101
N	100 1110	n	110 1110
O	100 1111	o	110 1111
P	101 0000	p	111 0000
Q	101 0001	q	111 0001
R	101 0010	r	111 0010
S	101 0011	s	111 0011
T	101 0100	t	111 0100
U	101 0101	u	111 0101
V	101 0110	v	111 0110
W	101 0111	w	111 0111
X	101 1000	x	111 1000
Y	101 1001	y	111 1001
Z	101 1010	z	111 1010
0	011 0000	!	010 0001
1	011 0001	"	010 0010
2	011 0010	#	010 0011
3	011 0011	%	010 0101
4	011 0100	&	010 0110
5	011 0101	:	011 1010
6	011 0110	<	011 1100
7	011 0111	>	011 1110
8	011 1000	?	011 1111
9	011 1001	@	100 0000
blank	000 0000	£	101 1100
(	010 1000	↑	101 1110
+	010 1011	—	101 1111
}	101 1101	blank	010 0000
{	101 1011		
$	010 0100		
*	010 1010		
)	010 1001		
;	011 1011		
,	010 1100		
–	010 1101		
=	011 1101		
.	010 1110		

Fig. 10.2. The ASCII code

Either with suitable hardware, or by the use of a suitable program subroutine in the microcomputer monitor, the pressing of a particular key on the keyboard can be detected and converted into the appropriate ASCII code for transmission along the data bus. The monitor program can also scroll the line up one when it is full and move the cursor to the start of the new line. The cursor is a symbol that indicates where the next input will be displayed. It is often a ■ or a —. The characters are made up from a matrix of dots. The common ones are seven rows by five columns and nine rows by seven columns.

The first character generators only produced 7 × 5 founts because of the amount of memory required by character generators. Each dot has to be stored in ROM as either a 1 for a bright spot on the TV screen or as a 0 for a blank. However, present MOSFET ROMs have allowed much greater memory on a single chip and 128-character, 9 × 7 fount, single chip character generators (8 K bit) are now common. When used with TV displays (horizontal scan) and printers each row of the character is presented at the parallel outputs of the character generator. These are then fed into a shift register, serialised, and used to control the television tube beam or the printer mechanism (printed black dot = logic 1).

In one method of visual display, software determines which character is to be output and where on the screen it is placed. The screen is divided into a convenient number of lines and each line into a convenient number of spaces for characters. Blank spaces are left at the start and end of each line to act as margins because most domestic televisions overscan. (This means that the start and end of each line are lost at the edges of the TV tube.) This can be corrected in some televisions by altering the width control.

A position in memory is allocated to each character position on the screen. The ASCII code for the character to be displayed has to be read into the correct position in this memory and is then read into the character generator at the correct time. This is known as a memory-mapped visual display.

Any external device can be addressed in this way and portions of memory can be dedicated to particular I/O devices. However, if the microprocessor also possesses input/output instructions and an input/output request facility then memory mapping of I/O is not necessary.

How does the microprocessor talk to external devices?

In previous chapters mention has been made of how external serial devices can be interfaced to the microcomputer by means of suitable interface adapters which contain shift registers and, perhaps, also buffers or electrical level translators to interface circuits from different logic families, e.g. MOS to TTL or to mechanical relays and other devices.

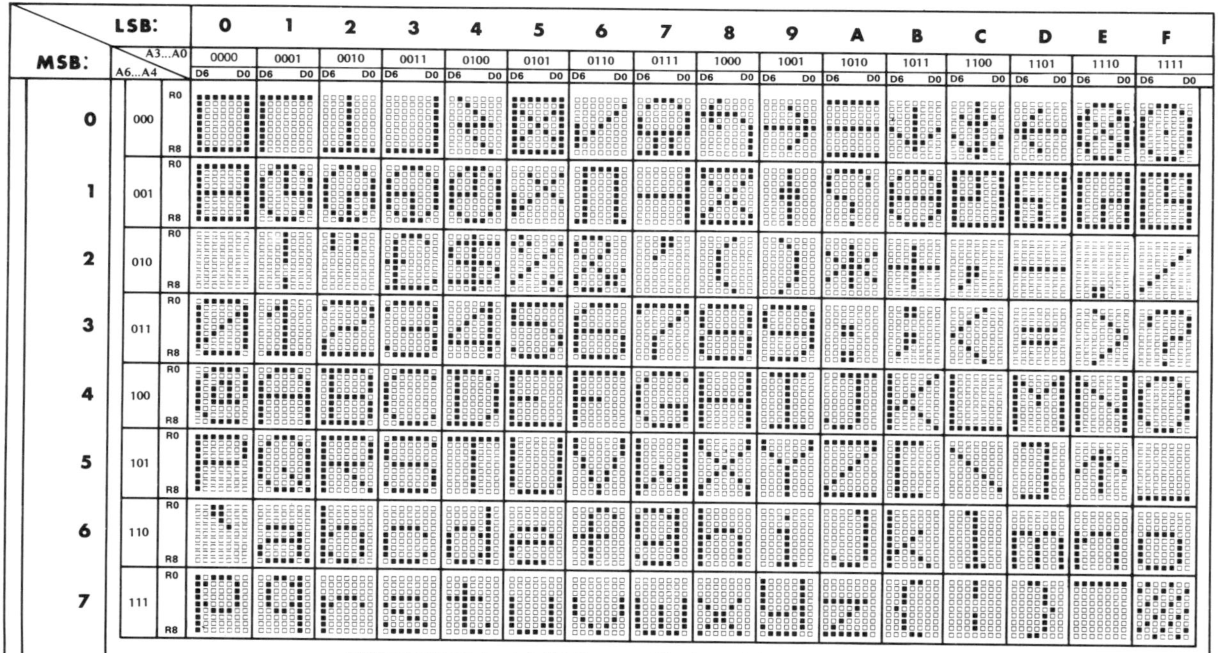

Fig. 10.3. A character fount

* Shifted character. The character is shifted three rows to R3 at the top end of the font and R11 at the bottom

121

These interface adapters can often be programmed themselves. In microcomputers transmission of data between external devices and the computer is usually asynchronous transfer – sometimes also called handshaking I/O. If the bits for each ASCII character were sent out in a long string then the microcomputer would have to be synchronised to the sending device in order for it to keep count of when one character ended and the next began. To overcome this difficult timing problem asynchronous transmission uses start and stop control bits at the beginning and end of each character. These keep the receiver in step with the sending device by making the receiver stop after receipt of each character and wait for the start of the next.

A typical arrangement when sending an eight bit word would be to have one extra start bit and one extra stop bit making ten bits in all. If the rate of bit transfer was 200 bits per second then the baud rate would be $8 \times 20 = 160$ baud because during each second there would also be 20 start and 20 stop bits which are not counted in the baud rate.

An asynchronous communications interface adapter (ACIA) can convert received serial data, start, stop and error detecting bits (if sent) to parallel data output, verify error-free data transmission and can generate interrupt signals. It can also convert parallel data from the data bus into serial form and generate and add the special start bits (usually one) and stop bits (usually one, one and a half, or two) and any error checking (parity) bits if required.

A universal asynchronous receiver and transmitter (UART) can similarly transmit and receive asynchronous serial data in *all* common formats.

Parallel input/output (PIO) interfaces may also be programmable and may contain several parallel registers acting as output ports as well as logic for interrupts.

When sending data from one device to another it is possible for errors to occur – often due to electrical noise on the line. For this reason some sort of check is often used to see if the data received is the same as the data sent.

One such method is known as a checksum. Suppose we wish to transmit a series of consecutive eight-bit words. We can split them into equal groups, add the words in each group to each other and send the least significant eight bits of the sum of each group after the group as a checksum. In practice the complement of the checksum is sent. When the data is received the checksum is recalculated and the value of the least significant eight bits, contained in the accumulator, added to the received value to see if there have been any errors

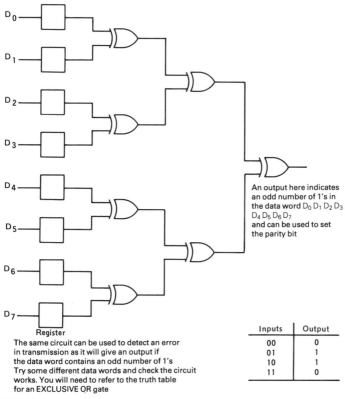

An output here indicates
an odd number of 1's in
the data word $D_0\ D_1\ D_2\ D_3$
$D_4\ D_5\ D_6\ D_7$
and can be used to set
the parity bit

Register

The same circuit can be used to detect an error
in transmission as it will give an output if
the data word contains an odd number of 1's
Try some different data words and check the circuit
works. You will need to refer to the truth table
for an EXCLUSIVE OR gate

Inputs	Output
00	0
01	1
10	1
11	0

Fig. 10.4. A simple parity bit generator for even parity

in transmission. The answer obtained should always be $1111\ 1111_2$
because for each digit $Q_i + \bar{Q}_i = 1$.

Some codes allow an error in a single byte to be detected. Such a
code is the parity check. An extra 'parity bit' is added to each
character sent and can be arranged so that the total number of 1s,
including the parity bit, in each word is even. See Fig. 10.4. On
receipt of the character it is checked and if the total number of 1s is
not even then the character is rejected and an error message is sent.
Sometimes odd parity is used. That is, the total number of 1s in each
character is arranged to be an odd number.

Microcomputers are so reliable compared with older types of
computers that error-checking codes are not used for 'internal' data
transfer but only for communication with external devices.

Sometimes synchronous transmission is employed between the
MPU and a device such as a floppy disk controller. No start and

123

stop bits are used and the peripheral has to be synchronised to the MPU.

A universal synchronous/asynchronous receiver-transmitter (USART) is a device capable of converting parallel data into virtually any serial transmission format required, synchronous or asynchronous.

11
A brief introduction to further programming techniques

We have already seen that the feature of a microcomputer that makes it so powerful is its ability not only to follow a fixed sequence of instructions but its ability to jump out of sequence, either unconditionally, or conditionally if certain circumstances are met.

How can the microprocessor be made to jump in a program?

The following types of instructions are usually available and can be used in a program to bring about a jump:

BRANCH (unconditional) – this instruction causes the program counter to be set directly to a non-sequential address in memory. The next instruction is therefore fetched from this non-sequential address. (Also called JUMP unconditional.)

BRANCH (conditional) – if the particular condition referred to in the instruction is met (usually a test to see if a particular flag is set) then the program counter is changed to a non-sequential address. The next instruction is fetched from this non-sequential address. (Also called JUMP conditional.)

CALL subroutine – the program counter is incremented and the address of the next instruction stored in the stack. This is the return address from the subroutine. The program counter is then loaded with the address of the subroutine and execution proceeds.

CONDITIONAL CALL subroutine – depends on the status of the appropriate condition flag.

RETURN – this causes the return address in the stack to pop and be loaded into the program counter so that the original program can continue on return from the subroutine.

CONDITIONAL RETURN – depends on the status of the appropriate condition flag.

How would I go about writing a complex program?

The steps in producing a program can be summarised as:

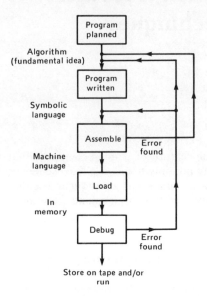

When programming in a high level language assembly and loading are taken care of for you. Monitor programs usually help with the debugging of programs.

The first step in writing the program is to formulate the fundamental idea called the program's algorithm. We have already examined a program to add two numbers. Suppose we now want to add all the numbers 1 to 200, i.e. $0 + 1 + 2 + 3 + ... + 199 + 200$. To do this directly would require a very large number of steps and be tedious to write. We can, however, devise a program using branching that will reduce the number of steps we have to write in the program.

The algorithm of the required program could be expressed as: 'We wish to obtain a result called SUM. We have a number called N. Both SUM and N are first made equal to zero. We then find SUM + N and call this NEW SUM. We then find N + 1, and test to see if it is less than 201. If it is, the process is repeated. If N + 1 is equal to 201 the program stops and the value of SUM is the required result.'

Algorithms are often better understood if represented as a diagram called a flow chart.

Note the shapes used:

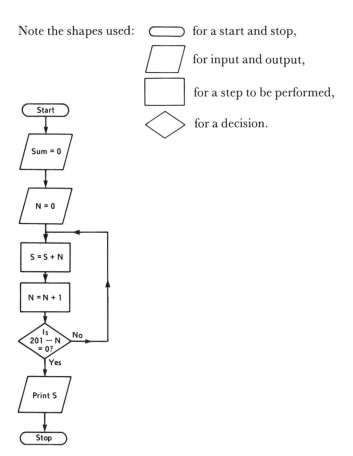

⬭ for a start and stop,

▱ for input and output,

▭ for a step to be performed,

◇ for a decision.

How is this flow chart converted into a program?

As a program in BASIC this could be:

```
10 LET S = 0
20 LET N = 0
30 LET S = S + N
40 LET N = N + 1
50 IF N<201 GO TO 30
60 PRINT S
70 END
```

When the program is run the answer is printed out.

At this point let us list all the instructions that we have so far examined for our hypothetical microprocessor described in the text. Then we can see if we can write a similar program for it in hexidecimal:

Instructions so far:

Description	Mnemo-nic	Symbolic operation
LOAD accumulator	LDA	$M \rightarrow A$
ADD without carry	ADD	$M + A \rightarrow A$
ADD with carry	ADC	$M + A + CF \rightarrow A$
STORE accumulator	STA	$A \rightarrow M$
INCREMENT accumulator	INC	$A + 1 \rightarrow A$
COMPLEMENT accumulator	COMP	$\bar{A} \rightarrow A$
AND memory and accumulator	AND	$M \cdot A \rightarrow A$
OR memory and accumulator	OR	$M + A \rightarrow A$
XOR memory and accumulator	XOR	$M \oplus A \rightarrow A$
CLEAR CARRY FLAG	CCF	$0 \rightarrow CF$
CLEAR ACCUMULATOR	CLA	$0 \rightarrow A$
SHIFT accumulator right	SAR	$0 \rightarrow \boxed{76543210} \rightarrow CF$
SHIFT accumulator left	SAL	$CF \leftarrow \boxed{76543210} \leftarrow 0$
STOP	BRK	PC stops.

where M is a memory location
A is the accumulator
CF is the carry flag
PC is the program counter.

The flags that we have mentioned so far have been the carry flag, the zero flag, the overflow flag and the sign, or negative, flag. These will be set or reset, as appropriate, according to the result of each arithmetic or logic operation performed. For instance, an ADD operation will:

1. Set the carry flag if there is a carry out from bit 7 of the result and reset it if there is no carry out.

2. Set the zero flag if the result is zero and reset it if the result is not zero.

3. Set the overflow flag if bit 7 of the result is different from bit 7 of either operand, and reset the overflow flag if not.

4. Set the sign flag if bit 7 of the result is a 1 – signifying a signed negative number – and reset the sign flag if bit 7 of the result is a 0 – signifying a signed positive number.

When using a real microprocessor you should examine the instruction set carefully to discover what flags are provided, and which instructions affect which flags, as this differs from one microprocessor type to another.

The information about which instructions affect which flags is usually presented as a table. Here is a table for our hypothetical microprocessor:

Operation	Mnemonic	Flags affected C	Z	O	S
LOAD accumulator	LDA	●	●	●	●
ADD without carry	ADD	*	*	*	*
ADD with carry	ADC	*	*	*	*
STORE accumulator	STA	●	●	●	●
INCREMENT accumulator	INC	●	●	●	●
COMPLEMENT accumulator	COMP	●	●	●	●
AND accumulator	AND	●	*	●	*
OR accumulator	OR	●	*	●	*
XOR accumulator	XOR	●	*	●	*
CLEAR CARRY FLAG	CCF	0	●	●	●
CLEAR ACCUMULATOR	CLA	0	1	0	0
SHIFT right	SAR	*	*	●	0
SHIFT left	SAL	*	*	●	*
STOP	BRK	●	●	●	●

Key ● flag not affected
0 flag reset to zero
1 flag set to 1
* flag set or reset according
to result of operation.
C = carry flag, Z = zero flag, O = overflow flag, S = sign flag

Let us now add three more instructions to our instruction set, none of which affects the flags. They are – BRANCH UNCON-DITIONALLY – BRANCH ON ZERO – BRANCH ON NOT ZERO. These instructions cause the program counter to jump to a specified value, either unconditionally or conditionally, depending on whether the zero flag is set, or not set, from a previous instruction.

Description	Mnemonic	Symbolic operation
BRANCH UNCONDITIONAL	BR	PC → ** **
BRANCH ON ZERO	BR Z	If zero flag set, PC → ** **
BRANCH ON NOT ZERO	BR NZ	If zero flag not set, PC → ** **

where ** ** is an address specified after the op-code and PC is the program counter.

Now let's see if we can convert our flow chart into a program. In using single precision arithmetic we would be in trouble because the answer (20100_{10}) is greater than the maximum unsigned number that can be stored in an eight-bit register. As we are only interested in this program as an example of how a flow chart is converted into a hex listing, and then in examining how these instructions control the computer, let's keep the arithmetic simple and only add the numbers 0 to 20. The final answer will then fit in an eight-bit register as an unsigned number. (An unsigned number means we do not bother to use bit 7 to indicate whether it is positive or negative, so this bit is available as part of the magnitude.) The flow chart is now:

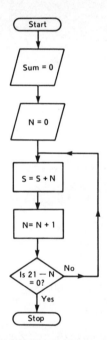

Represented as a list of instructions like those used in Chapter 3 for the conceptual 'rack' computer, the 'program' would be:

Location	Operation	Argument	Comments
000	LOAD	101	GET N
001	ADD without carry	102	NEW S = S + N
002	STORE	102	Store NEW S
003	LOAD	101	GET N

004	INC accumulator	–	N = N + 1
005	STORE	101	Store NEW N
006	COMP accumulator	–	⎰ 2s comp of
007	INC accumulator	–	⎱ NEW N
008	ADD without carry	100	21 – NEW N
009	BRANCH ON NOT ZERO	000	Loop till done
010	STOP	–	

100	This location is loaded with the number 21
101	This location is loaded with the first value of N (= 0)
102	This location is loaded with the first value of S (= 0)

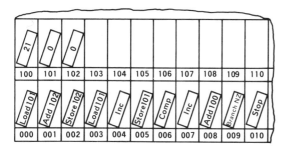

Fig. 11.1. Conceptual 'rack' model

There is no print instruction. Instead, after the program has been run, the memory location 102 is examined to find the answer.

This program could be written in assembly mnemonics as:

Label	Operand	Argument
START	LDA	101
	ADD	102
	STA	102
	LDA	101
	INC	
	STA	101
	COMP	
	INC	
	ADD	100
	BR NZ,	START
	BRK	

The addresses 100, 101 and 102 refer to our conceptual 'rack' computer. As far as any real microprocessor is concerned they are symbolic addresses and it is usual to give these names rather than to use numbers. We could write the assembly language program as:

Label	Operand argument	Comments
START	LDA, NUM STORE	GET N
	ADD, SUM STORE	NEW S = S + N
	STA, SUM STORE	STORE NEW SUM
	LDA, NUM STORE	GET N
	INC	N = N + 1
	STA, NUM STORE	STORE NEW N
	COMP	} 2s comp N
	INC	
	ADD, KEY STORE	21 – NEW N
	BR NZ, START	Do again from START
	BRK	STOP

How do I convert assembly language to hexadecimal?

First you need the list of hex op-codes for our hypothetical microprocessor.

Mnemonic	Op-code		
LDA	AD	**	**
ADD	6D	**	**
STA	8D	**	**
BR NZ	2B	**	**

These are three-byte instructions where ** ** is an address in memory from which data is either to be obtained or stored.

INC	16
COMP	17
BRK	00

These are one-byte instructions.

The hex program can now be assembled. Starting at the first instruction we can go through the program assigning a location to each instruction. If the first instruction op-code is placed at 0000_{16} then, as it is a three-byte instruction, the next instruction op-code will be at 0003_{16}.

If we go through all the instructions assigning hex locations to each we will end up with:

Location	Label	Operand argument
0000	START	LDA, NUM STORE
0003		ADD, SUM STORE
0006		STA, SUM STORE
0009		LDA, NUM STORE
000C		INC
000D		STA, NUM STORE
0010		COMP
0011		INC
0012		ADD, KEY STORE
0015		BR NZ, START
0018		BRK

Next an actual hex address has to be given to each symbolic address. We can see that START is 0000_{16}. The others – KEY STORE, SUM STORE, and NUM STORE – can be any address greater than 0018_{16}, (i.e. any address not so far used). Let's choose 0064_{16}, 0065_{16}, and 0066_{16}.

KEY STORE	EQU 0064
NUM STORE	EQU 0065
START	EQU 0000
SUM STORE	EQU 0066

The next step is to go through the program again and construct the instructions in hex (op-code and address if required) at each location. If your microcomputer will only handle binary then you must use binary instead of hex.

Locations	Contents (instructions)
0000	AD 65 00
0003	6D 66 00
0006	8D 66 00
0009	AD 65 00
000C	16
000D	8D 65 00
0010	17
0011	16
0012	6D 64 00
0015	2B 00 00
0018	00

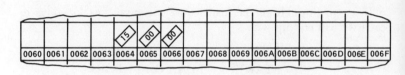

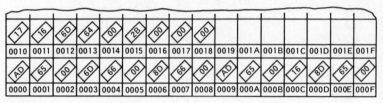

Fig. 11.2 The conceptual 'rack' model with hexadecimal codes

The first value of N (i.e. zero) has to be stored at 0065_{16}, the first value of S (i.e. zero) at 0066_{16}, and the number 21_{10} at 0064_{16}:

0064	15
0065	00
0066	00

Note: the hex value of 21_{10} is 15_{16}. This is shown in Fig. 11.2.

How is this program run, and what actually takes place inside the microprocessor?

The program counter is set to the location of the first instruction (0000_{16}) and when the program is run the first instruction op-code AD_{16} is fetched from this location, followed by the address (least significant byte first), from locations 0002_{16} and 0003_{16}, as and when indicated by the program counter. When this instruction is executed the first value of N (i.e. zero) which is stored at memory location 0065_{16} is loaded into the accumulator.

The next op-code $6D_{16}$ and the address 0066_{16} are then fetched in a similar way and when this instruction is executed the first value of S (i.e. zero) which is stored in memory location 0066_{16} is added to N in the accumulator.

The result S + N (still zero at this point) is the NEW SUM and will now be in the accumulator. The next instruction 8D 66 00 is now fetched and when executed stores the NEW SUM back at location 0066_{16} in place of the old value of S. The instruction AD 65 00 is next fetched and, when executed, the first value of N, still stored at location 0065_{16}, is placed in the accumulator in place of the number already there.

The next instruction fetched is INC accumulator, 16_{16}, and this causes N to be incremented by one. The accumulator now holds the second value of N (i.e. N + 1) called NEW N. When the next instruction is fetched, 8D 65 00, and executed, the new value of N is stored back in memory in place of the old value in location 0065_{16}.

The accumulator still holds this new value of N, because it has not been changed since the INC instruction. The next instruction fetched and executed, 17_{16}, complements the contents of the accumulator. The instruction after that, 16_{16}, adds one to the accumulator. The accumulator now holds the 2s complement of the second value of N. (Complement + 1 = 2s complement.)

The next instruction, 6D 64 00, adds the number stored in loction 0064_{16} to the accumulator. This is the number 21_{10}. The next instruction, 2B 00 00, tests the zero flag and causes the program counter to jump to 0000_{16} if the last instruction has not set the zero flag (i.e. NEW N was less than 21_{10}). The instruction at 0000_{16} is now fetched. This is the first instruction again, but the value of N now fetched is the NEW N and will be 1.

The program is looped through repeatedly with N and S increasing until eventually the NEW N is equal to 21_{10}, at which point the number stored as SUM is the required answer. The BRANCH IF NOT ZERO fails and the program counter will be incremented to 0018_{16}. When the instruction at this location, 00_{16}, is fetched the program stops and if the memory location 0066_{16} is read the required answer is found.

This example has served to show *how* a 'typical' microprocessor *functions* and how a program can be written. Unfortunately there is no such thing as a true typical microprocessor and the hypothetical microprocessor has been kept very general so as to cover as many aspects of the working of a real microprocessor as possible. Some microprocessors only have add with carry instructions, some do not have clear accumulator instructions. All common real microprocessors have a single instruction for subtract that replaces the instructions COMP, INC, ADD when you want to subtract. Beware – the 6502 only has a 'subtract with borrow' ($A - M - \overline{CF} \rightarrow A$). If you want to subtract without borrow you have to set the carry flag first. Others have subtract with carry ($A - M - CF \rightarrow A$) and subtract without carry ($A - M \rightarrow A$).

If you are going to program in a low level language, you should first study the instruction set for the microprocessor you are using to discover what instructions, and what addressing modes, are available. Not all instructions will be available in all addressing modes.

Both the actual instructions, and the addressing modes provided, are different for different microprocessor types.

At first you will be confused by so many instructions and will probably write very inefficient programs, but you will soon get used to your particular microprocessor instruction set. You will find there are several ways to tackle any particular program and if you are short of memory space you will have to make the most economical use of the instructions that are available to you.

The hypothetical microprocessor described in the text was given a very simple instruction set. Real microprocessors provide single instructions that enable you to carry out such operations as decrementing, incrementing and shifting of not only the accumulator but also of the contents of other MPU registers and sometimes of memory locations as well. This means that less movement of data is required and programs can be kept shorter.

For instance, if instructions are provided to clear the accumulator (CLA), and to decrement the contents of a memory location (DEC) $M-1 \rightarrow M$, then, provided the result of the decrement memory affects the zero flag, a program to add all the numbers from 0 to 20 could be written as:

Label	Operand argument	Comments
START	CLA	S = 0
LOOP	ADD, NUM STORE	ADD N
	DEC, NUM STORE	NEXT N
	BR NZ, LOOP	LOOP IF NEXT N not zero
	STA, ANSWER	STORE answer
	BRK	STOP

The number 20 is placed in location NUM STORE and the program can then be run. The answer will be found in memory location ANSWER.

A flow chart for this program would be:

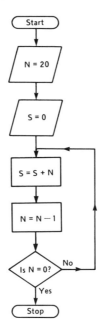

Real microprocessors allow the use of several different addressing modes and, when writing in assembly language, a distinction has to be made between data that is to be used immediately and memory addresses whose contents are to be used. One method of distinguishing between them is to use the symbol # to indicate an immediate data value. For example LDA, # NUM would mean load the actual value NUM, but LDA, NUM STORE would mean load the number stored at the address NUM STORE. Another common method uses brackets. LDA, NUM means load the actual value NUM, but LDA, (NUM STORE) means load the number stored at the address NUM STORE.

Appendix 1
Glossary of terms

Access time. Time taken for a particular byte of storage to become available.

ACIA. *A*synchronous *C*ommunication *I*nterface *A*dapter.

Acoustic coupler. Connects a modulated output, e.g. from a MODEM, to an audio frequency device such as a telephone without having to make electrical connections.

Accumulator. The register in the microprocessor asociated with arithmetic and logic manipulation. The results of these manipulations are usually presented in the accumulator register.

Address. An identification that designates a particular location – usually in memory.

ALGOL. *ALGO*rithmic *L*anguage; a high level programming language.

Algorithm. The set of rules for solving a problem in a finite number of operations.

Alphanumeric. Letters and number characters, usually taken to include other symbols as well.

ALU. See **arithmetic and logic unit.**

APL. *A P*rogramming *L*anguage.

Architecture. Any design or orderly arrangement.

Arithmetic and logic unit (ALU). The part of the microprocessor that performs the arithmetic and logic operations.

ASCII. *A*merican *S*tandard *C*ode for *I*nformation *I*nterchange. A binary code used to represent letters, numbers, etc.

Assembler. A machine language program that translates human coded instructions (mnemonics) into binary information (machine language) for the computer to use.

Assembly language. A code for representing program statements in mnemonics that can be conveniently handled by humans and the assembly program.

Asynchronous. Operations that initiate a new operation immediately upon completion of the current one regardless of the rest of the system; not synchronised.

Background. The execution of lower priority programs during periods when the system resources are not required for the higher priority foreground program.

Backing store. A large capacity store in addition to the working memory; tape cassettes or floppy disks.

Backplane. A board carrying the system bus into which the other parts of the computer can be connected; also called a mother board.

Banking. See **memory banking.**

BASIC. *B*eginners *A*ll-purpose *S*ymbolic *I*nstruction *C*ode; a high level programming language.

Baud. A measure of the speed of data flow; the number of bits of data sent per second.

BCD. *B*inary *C*oded *D*ecimal; a method of representing decimal numbers where *each* decimal digit is represented by its binary equivalent.

Benchmark. A common task for the implementation of which programs can be written for different microprocessors in order to compare the efficiency of the different MPUs in a particular application.

Binary. A base 2 number system using only the digits 0 and 1.

Bipolar transistor. A conventional transistor in which the controlled current passes through two types of semiconductor, N and P.

Bit. A single *BI*nary digi*T*, i.e. 0 or 1.

Bootstrap. A method of loading a complex monitor into a computer by first using a small routine in ROM to enable more complex ones to be read in.

Branch. The capability of a microprocessor to modify the program sequence.

Breakpoint. A program address at which execution halts to allow debugging or data entry.

Bubble memory. A magnetic memory that does not forget even when the power is turned off. Midway in price and speed between PROM and floppy disk.

Buffer. Circuit to provide electrical isolation between parts of a system, or to match impedances, though data can still flow.

Bug. An error in the hardware or software of a computer.

Bus. A network of paths for data, control, power etc.

Bus driver. An IC added to the data bus to provide proper drive to the MPU when several memories are all connected to the data bus.

Byte. A group of eight bits.

CAI. *C*omputer *A*ided *I*nstruction.

Card. A printed circuit board.

Central processing unit (CPU). The heart of any computer system where the arithmetic logic and control functions are performed.

Checksum. A method of checking for errors in transmission of data. It is the least significant eight bits of the summation of a group of words sent together as a group. The checksum is complemented and sent after the group. Upon reception the checksum is calculated again and, when added to the complemented checksum that was transmitted, will give the answer $1111\ 1111_2$, provided there were no errors in transmission.

Chip. The tiny silicon slices used to make electronic circuits.

Circuit board. A rigid card on which various electronic parts are mounted. Printed or etched copper tracks connect the various parts.

Clock. The master timing circuit for a microprocessor that synchronises all its operations.

CMOS. *C*omplementary *M*etal *O*xide *S*emiconductor.

COBAL. *CO*mmon *A*lgorithmic *L*anguage; a structured high level language.

COBOL. *CO*mmon *B*usiness *O*riented *L*anguage; a high level programming language.

Code. A set of rules outlining the way in which data may be represented. Often used to mean language, as in machine code meaning machine language.

Compiler. A program that converts high level language statements into either assembly language statements or into machine language which can then be run on the computer. The compiler is capable of replacing single-source program statements with a series of machine language instructions or with a subroutine. Contrast with **interpreter**.

CORAL. *C*omputer *O*n-line *R*eal-time *A*pplication *L*anguage. This is a development of ALGOL, a high level language.

Counter. A register whose contents are used to represent the number of occurrences of an event.

CPU. See **Central Processing Unit.**

Cross-assembler. The program that enables a microprocessor to produce the machine language program for a microprocessor with a different instruction set.

CRT. *C*athode *R*ay *T*ube; TV display tube.

Cursor. A moving character displayed to show where the next output will be printed.

CUTS. *C*omputer *U*sers' *T*ape *S*ystem. Definition of a system for storing data on cassette tape as a series of tones to represent binary 1s and 0s.

Data. Facts or unevaluated messages, e.g. in a microcomputer, 1s and 0s. They are not in themselves information; see **information.**

Data bus. The system of lines for transmission of data both inside and outside the microprocessor.

Debug. To correct errors.

Dedicated. A microprocessor that has been specifically, and often permanently, programmed for a single application, e.g. TV games, traffic control.

Digital. Deals in discrete data as distinct from continuously variable information such as an analogue device.

DIL. *D*ual-*I*n-*L*ine.

DIP. *D*ual-*I*n-*L*ine *P*ackage.

Direct addressing. An addressing mode where the address of the operand is contained in the instruction after the operation code.

Disk (disc). See **floppy disk.**

Diskette. See **floppy disk.**

DMA. *D*irect *M*emory *A*ccess. A method by which data can be transferred between peripheral devices and internal memory without intervention by the microprocessor.

DOS. *D*isk *O*perating *S*ystem. A monitor program to obtain data from, manage and service, files stored on floppy disks.

Driver. A software driver is a series of instructions the computer follows to reformat data for transfer to and from a particular peripheral. For a hardware driver see **bus driver.**

Dumb terminal. A peripheral without any intelligence of its own.

Dump. To transfer to a backing store such as tape or floppy disk.

Duplex. Transfer of data between two devices in two directions at the same time.

Dynamic memory. RAM memory that needs to be refreshed every few milliseconds.

EAROM. *E*lectrically *A*lterable *R*ead *O*nly *M*emory.

EBCDIC. An eight-bit data code along the same lines as ASCII.

Edit. To arrange data into the format required for subsequent processing.

Environment. The conditions of all registers, flags, etc. at any instant in a program.

EPROM. *E*rasable *P*rogrammable *R*ead *O*nly *M*emory.

Execute. To perform a sequence of program steps.

Execution time. The time taken to perform an instruction, often quoted as so many clock cycles (T states).

Executive routine. A master program that controls the execution of other programs, e.g. the monitor.

FET. *F*ield *E*ffect *T*ransistor.

Field. (1) A group of related characters treated as a unit. (2) The background on a visual display, e.g. reverse field, black on white background instead of white on black background.

FIFO. *F*irst-*In*-*F*irst-*O*ut.

File. A collection of related records treated as a unit, stored on tape or floppy disk.

Firmware. Software stored permanently in ROM, PROM or EPROM.

Fixed point. A convention used to represent non-integer (fractional) numbers; see also **floating point.**

Flag. A flip-flop that may be set or reset under software control to indicate some special condition.

Flag register. A register made up of several one bit flags; see **status register.**

Flip-flop. Electronic two state device used to store binary digits.

Floating point. A convention for representing a non-integer number using scientific exponential notation.

Floppy disk. A flexible plastic disk coated with the same magnetic material used for recording tape. The disk is used for mass storage of data in tracks on its surface.

Flow chart. A diagram representing the logic of a computer program.

Foreground. A priority program, the main program; see **background.**

FORTRAN. *FOR*mula *TRAN*slation; a high level programming language.

Gate. An electronic circuit that is either ON or OFF depending on its inputs. The building block of computers.

Glitch. A noise (unwanted) pulse.

Handshaking. A means by which a peripheral and the microprocessor can report their status during data transfer.

Hard copy. Permanent printout on paper.

Hardware. The actual electronic and mechanical parts of a computer.

Hardwire. Logic gates wired together in such a way that the wiring pattern determines the overall logic operation.

Hash. (1) Continuous noise signal. (2) The # sign.

Hexadecimal. A base 16 number system using the digits 0 to 9 and A, B, C, D, E, F.

High level language. An easy-to-use programming language that is closer to the needs of the problem to be solved than to the binary input needs of the computer.

Highway. Synonymous with bus.

IC. Integrated circuit.

Immediate addressing. Addressing mode that contains the operand in the instruction.

Indexed addressing. A form of indirect addressing using an index register.

Indirect addressing. An addressing mode in which the instruction contains the address of the location where the address of the operand may be found.

Information. The meaning assigned to data by humans.

Initialise. To set up all registers, flags, etc. to defined conditions.

Input. The means by which data is entered into a computer – keyboard or switches; the act of entering data; the actual data entered.

Instruction. Bit pattern which must be supplied to the microprocessor to cause it to perform a particular operation. Common instructions consist of an op-code on its own or an op-code plus data or an op-code plus the address of data.

Instruction register. Microprocessor register used to hold instruction op-codes fetched from memory.

Instruction set. The repertoire of instructions for an MPU.

Integer. A whole number – positive, negative or zero.

Intelligent terminal. A computer peripheral capable of computing operations on its own.

Interface. A circuit that controls the flow and format of data between the microprocessor and peripherals.

Interpreter. A program that translates each high level language statement into a sequence of machine instructions and then executes those machine instructions before translating the next high level language statement, in contrast to a compiler which produces the entire machine language program before executing it.

Interrupt. A signal that interrupts a running program so that some other task can be performed. Interrupts are sometimes given priorities – a non-maskable interrupt is always serviced immediately. An interrupt mask bit prevents the MPU from responding to maskable interrupt requests until cleared by execution of programmed instructions.

I/O. Input/output.

Job. A collection of specified tasks.

Jump. Synonymous with branch.

K. Kilo; a thousand, but often used to mean $2^{10} = 1024$, particularly when used as kilobyte (K byte) which is 1024 bytes.

Kansas City. Definition of a CUTS-based cassette interface system.

Keyboard. A panel of switches or push-buttons used to enter programs and data.

Label. One or more characters used to identify a program statement or a data item.

Language. A system of programming instructions understood by both the programmer and the computer. Machine language instructions vary from one microprocessor to another but high level languages such as BASIC can be used, with minor variations, on different computers with BASIC interpreters.

Latch. A flip-flop that retains the previous input state until overwritten.

Library. A collection of programs written for a particular computer or microprocessor.

Library routine. A tested routine maintained in a library of programs.

LIFO._Last-In-First-Out_ stack; an area of memory set aside for temporary storage.

Light pen. A means of input of data, drawings, etc. by means of a sensor that is held in contact with the VDU screen.

Line printer. A printer that prints out results a line at a time in contrast to a normal printer that prints one character at a time.

Look ahead. A feature of adders and ALUs that allows them to look ahead to see that all carries generated are available. It is also applied to the feature of a CPU that allows it to mask an interrupt request until the next instruction has been completed.

Look-up tables. Information stored in memory. The answer can be looked-up by the MPU instead of the calculation having to be performed.

Looping. A programming technique where one section of the program (the loop) is performed many times over.

LSI. _Large Scale Integration_; more than 100 components per chip.

Machine language. A language used directly by the microprocessor; no interpreter is required.

Macro instruction. A source-language instruction that is equivalent to a specified number of machine language instructions.

Mainframe. Colloquially used to refer to the large original computers that required a main framework to house the various parts of their central processing units.

Megabytes. 1 million bytes (MB).

Memory. The part of a system which stores data.

Memory banking. a method of enlarging a microcomputer's memory to more than 64 K bytes by using banks of 64 K byte memory cards selected one at a time by use of chip enable inputs.

Memory map. Chart showing the memory allocations of a system.

Memory mapped I/O. A technique of implementing I/O facilities by addressing I/O ports as if they were memory locations.

Menu. A multichoice question displayed by the program, e.g. 'What do you want to do? (1) Play games (2) Accounts (3) Appointments.'

MHz. Mega Hertz; 1 million cycles per second.

Microcomputer. A computer made by combining a microprocessor with some memory.

Micro cycle. Single program step in an MPU's microprogram; one machine program step.

Microprocessor. A complete central processing unit on one chip, implemented by the use of a large scale integrated circuit.

Microprogram. The program inside the MPU which controls the MPU chip during its fetch/execute sequence.

Mini floppy. See **floppy disk.**

Mini computer. A small computer more powerful than a microcomputer; often does not use a microprocessor but uses discrete logic chips.

Mnemonic. A word, or series of letters, that stands for another longer word or phrase and is easier to remember.

MODEM. *MO*dulator/*DEM*odulator used to send and receive serial data over an audio line. It is illegal to make electrical connections to a telephone line so an acoustic coupler is then also required.

Monitor. A program, usually stored in ROM, that gives a computer its fundamental interactive intelligence. The monitor contains software routines and I/O drivers needed by the user to operate the system. Sometimes referred to as the executive routine. It tells the computer how and where to acquire the programs and data, where to store them and how to run them.

Motherboard. See **backplane.**

MSI. *M*edium *S*cale *I*ntegration; between 10 and 100 components per chip.

Multiplexing. A system of transmitting data from several devices over a single line.

Natural language. A human language such as English.

Negative logic. The opposite of positive logic; 0 is represented by $V+$ and 1 by zero volts.

Nibble. A four-bit word.

NRZ. *N*on *R*eturn to Zero; a method of coding digital information on magnetic tape.

NMOS. *N*-type *M*etal *O*xide *S*emiconductor.

Non-volatile. Memory that will retain data even when the power is switched off.

Object code. Machine language program instructions.

Object program. Machine language program.

O/C. *O*pen *C*ollector; a means of tying together outputs from several TTL devices on the same bus, similar to TSO in MOS.

Octal. The base eight number system.

Op-code. Operation code; a bit pattern that specifies a particular machine operation.

Operand. The data upon which the mathematical or logical operation is performed.

Operating system. A sophisticated monitor program often found with floppy disk system.

Output. The means by which data leaves a computer, e.g. printer, VDU; the act of outputting data; the data itself that is output.

Parallel. Transfer of two or more bits at the same time.

Parity. A check bit added to data can give odd or even parity to act as a check for error in transmitted data. In odd parity there are an odd number of 1s per word, in even parity an even number of 1s.

Patch. To modify a routine in an expedient way.

Peripheral. Any accessory that can be added to a computer to increase its capability.

Personal computer. An economical microcomputer designed for use by one individual, as distinct from larger computers which are usually designed to be shared.

PIA. *P*eripheral *I*nterface *A*dapter.

Pilot. *P*rogrammed *I*nquiry *L*earnings *O*r *T*eachings; a high level language developed for CAI.

PIO. *P*arallel *I*nput *O*utput controller.

PL/1. *P*rogramming *L*anguage *1* – a high level language.

PMOS. *P*-type *M*etal *O*xide *S*emiconductor.

Polling. A method used to identify the source of interrupt requests and enable the control program to decide which to service first.

Pop. To remove a word from the stack.

Port. The communication line and terminal through which the MPU communicates with the outside world.

Program. The list of instructions or statements that tells the computer what to do.

Program counter. A register that holds the address of the next part of the program to be executed.

Programmer. (1) A person who writes programs. (2) The hardware for programming electrical programmable read only memory. (PROM).

PROM. *P*rogrammable *R*ead *O*nly *M*emory.

Prompt. A character displayed by a computer as a signal that it expects a response.

Push. The operation of putting data on to the stack.

QWERTY. Refers to the first six letters on a full typewriter keyboard; used to signify a full keyboard.

Radix. The base of a number system, e.g. decimal is base 10, binary base 2.

RAM. *R*andom *A*ccess *M*emory; used to designate memory that may be written into and read out from any location. Random access implies that the access time is the same for every location.

Random Access Memory. See **RAM.**

Real-time clock. A piece of hardware that interrupts the microprocessor at fixed time intervals to synchronise its operations with events occurring in the outside world.

Real-time operation. A technique used to allow the computer to utilise information as it becomes available; data is processed quickly enough to produce output to control, direct, or affect the outcome of an ongoing activity or process.

Refresh. A signal sent to dynamic RAM every few milliseconds to enable it to refresh its contents.

Register. General purpose or dedicated MPU storage location; usually holds one word.

Relative addressing. An addressing mode where the address of the operand is formed by combining the contents of the program counter with an address (displacement) contained in the instruction.

Relocate. To place somewhere else in memory.

RF modulator. Converts video output to an output suitable for connecting to the aerial socket of a domestic TV.

ROM. *R*ead *O*nly *M*emory; this is pre-programmed and is only read from during use. It is random access and can be read out from any location.

Routine. An ordered set of general use instructions for use within a program.

RS232. A standard protocol for serial communications between computers and peripheral devices.

Run. To execute a program.

Scratch pad. Memory that has a short access time and is used by the system for short term data storage, often of intermediate results.

Serial. Transfer of data one bit at a time; contrast with **parallel.**

Simplex. Data transmission between two devices in one direction at a time only.

Simulation. A program that is used to represent or analyse the properties or behaviour of a real or a hypothetical system. Simulators are used to debug object code generated by a cross-assembler on a microprocessor other than the one being worked on.

Smart terminal. See **intelligent terminal.**

Software. The actual program.

Solid state. Electronic components whose operation depends on the control of electric or magnetic phenomena in solids, e.g. transistors and diodes.

SOS. *S*ilicon *O*n *S*apphire.

Source language. A program language other than machine language.

SSI. *S*mall *S*cale *I*ntegration; up to ten components per chip.

Stack. A block of successive memory locations accessible from one end (LIFO).

Stack pointer. A register that keeps track of the position of data stored in the stack.

Statement. A generalised instruction in high level language; several instructions on one line.

State of the art. Uses the latest technology.

Static memory. RAM that holds information without the need for refreshing for as long as the power remains on; more expensive than dynamic RAM.

Status register. A register that is used to store information on certain conditions related to data in the accumulator; also called a flag register.

String. A group of data elements stored in sequential memory locations and treated as one unit for program manipulations.

Subroutine. Part of a master program which performs an often-required task and can be called from any point in the main program.

Synchronous. In step with.

Syntax. The grammar of a programming language.

System. A complete computer made up of compatible hardware.

Terminal. An input device such as a keyboard; an output device such as a printer or a TV; or both.

Time sharing. A computer system that seems to be performing multiple tasks for a number of users simultaneously. In fact the microprocessor is only working for one user at any particular moment but its response is so fast compared with the user's response that he is not aware of this fact.

Transparent. Parts of the microprocessor such as the control flags and sometimes some of the registers, are said to be transparent to the programmer. This means he has no direct control over them.

Tri-state output (TSO). A chip output that can be made to go high impedance as well as to have outputs corresponding to logic 0 and 1.

T-state. One clock cycle.

Turnkey. A system that is ready to perform all tasks the moment you turn it on. No pre-programming by the user is required. Business systems are frequently supplied like this.

Two's complement arithmetic. System for handling negative numbers.

UART. *U*niversal *A*synchronous *R*eceiver and *T*ransmitter; an interface.

USART. *U*niversal *S*ynchronous/*A*synchronous *R*eceiver and *T*ransmitter.

User group. An association of persons who all own or operate similar or identical microcomputers (or equipment with the same microprocesor).

VDU. *V*isual *D*isplay *U*nit or *V*ideo *D*isplay *U*nit; TV screen.

Vector. Memory address directing the MPU to a new area of memory.

Vectored interrupt. A system in which each interrupt has its own uniquely recognisable address.

Video. Output suitable for connection to a video monitor (a TV set without an RF tuner).

VSLI. *V*ery *L*arge *S*cale *I*ntegration; more than 1000 components per chip.

Volatile. Memory devices that lose their data content if the power supply is switched off.

Word. A collection of binary digits treated as a unit and given a single location in memory.

Word length. The number of binary digits treated as a word. First generation microprocessors used four-bit words, second generation use eight-bit words, the latest microprocessors use 16-bit words.

Wordprocessor. Software, or combination of software and hardware, for manipulating text, e.g. inserting standard paragraphs, justifying right-hand margins, etc.

Appendix 2

Flowchart symbols

TERMINAL – indicates beginning and end of program.

AN ACTION OR PROCESS –

INPUT/OUTPUT – Data or results.

DECISION

CONNECTOR – used between pages when the flow chart takes more than one page.

CONNECTOR – used between different parts of the same page.

FLOWLINE

ANNOTATION FLAG – for adding comments.

PREPARATION

PREDEFINED PROCESS – e.g. SUB-ROUTINE.

System flowcharts

Sometimes people produce flowcharts to show, and analyse, the flow of data through their system. Such a system flowchart provides information on how the data is input and output. The symbol for Input and Output is therefore replaced with one whose shape suggests the type of input or output medium.

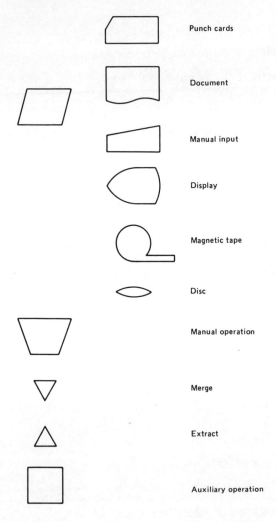

Punch cards

Document

Manual input

Display

Magnetic tape

Disc

Manual operation

Merge

Extract

Auxiliary operation

Index

154